Oakland
Hills

GRAND

BELLEVUE AVE.

LAKESIDE DR.

19TH
ST.

Lake
Merritt

LAKESHORE

Camron-
Stanford
House

Oakland, CA

Oakland
Library

12TH ST.

11TH ST.

10TH ST.

E. 12TH ST.

9TH ST.

Henry J.
Kaiser
Convention
Center

ALICE ST.

E. 10TH ST.

7TH ST.

880

Amtrak
Terminal

EMBARCADERO

©'03 Ja

Oakland Estuary

Blues City

WITHDRAWN

ALSO BY ISHMAEL REED

NOVELS

The Free-Lance Pallbearers

Yellow Back Radio Broke-Down

Mumbo Jumbo

The Last Days of Louisiana Red

Flight to Canada

The Terrible Twos

Reckless Eyeballing

The Terrible Threes

Japanese by Spring

ESSAYS

Another Day at the Front

The Reed Reader

Writin' Is Fightin'

God Made Alaska for the Indians

Shrovetide in Old New Orleans

Airing Dirty Laundry

Blues City

A WALK IN OAKLAND

979
.466054
R324b

Ishmael Reed

8/09

 CROWN JOURNEYS

CROWN PUBLISHERS · NEW YORK

Title spread photograph © Morton Beebe/CORBIS
Photograph on page 176 © Richard Nagler 2003

Published by Crown Journeys, an imprint of Crown Publishers, New York.
Member of the Crown Publishing Group, a division of Random House, Inc.
www.randomhouse.com

CROWN JOURNEYS and the Crown Journeys colophon are trademarks of
Random House, Inc.

Printed in the United States of America

Design by Lauren Dong
Map by Jackie Aher

Library of Congress Cataloging-in-Publication Data

Reed, Ishmael, 1938–
   Blues city : a walk in Oakland / Ishmael Reed.
   1. Oakland (Calif.)—Description and travel.   2. Oakland (Calif.)—
History.   3. Oakland (Calif.)—Social life and customs.   4. Reed, Ishmael,
1938—Journeys—California—Oakland.   5. Reed, Ishmael, 1938—
Homes and haunts—California—Oakland.   6. Walking—California—
Oakland.   I. Title.
   F869.O2R44 2003
   979.4'66054—dc21   2003006386

ISBN 1-4000-4540-1

First Edition

This book is dedicated to David McClure,
"The Gum Man."

Blues City

New York

U NLIKE OAKLAND WRITER Joaquin Miller, whose
The Destruction of Gotham (1886) painted a grim portrait of New York, or Jack London and George "the Greek"
Sterling, whose experiences in New York were depressing,
or Bret Harte, who went broke there after the novelty of
being a cowboy writer wore off, I was spoiled by New York.
Western writers, at least in the view of urbane easterners,
have usually been classified as cranks. Jack London, a socialist, cussed out some wealthy New Yorkers, and the western-
style dress of London and Joaquin Miller was viewed with
amused curiosity by New Yorkers. Much later, San Francisco
writer Richard Brautigan continued the tradition of wowing
easterners with frontier attire and manners. He'd be dressed
as a cowboy when I used to meet him at 1 Fifth Avenue in
Greenwich Village for lunch in the 1960s. This eccentricity
seemed to be provoked by the westerner's presence in the
hostile East.

But I had the opposite experience. It wasn't New York that frustrated me but San Francisco. In 1958, when I was twenty, I traveled to the city from my hometown of Buffalo in a beat-up car with two friends, an Italian-American named David and a Native American named Kirk. Kirk drove. Of course, we didn't know he was Native American until he slammed the brakes in anger when David, upon seeing some Native Americans on the street, remarked, "Look at those drunken Indians." Once the car had come to a sudden stop, Kirk said, "You've been seated next to one all day."

We hung around North Beach for a couple of months but, unable to find jobs, headed back to Buffalo. The police stopped us for speeding near North Platte, Nebraska, and arrested Kirk. We were stranded. David and I went to a local restaurant to figure out a plan when, overhearing our predicament, the strawberry-haired waitress told us to go to her house and have dinner. She said that her sister was home. I think that I must have been one of the few blacks in town, because as we were headed to the waitress's house, an Indian woman, sitting in a passing truck, pointed at me frantically. The driver, a black man, saw me and, with a startled look, began to wave. He waved until the truck was out of sight. I was a kind of celebrity, accorded the kind of treatment that black American celebrities received in Europe at the time—a combination of shock and fascination. It was an exciting week all around in North Platte: In addition to the presence of a second real, live black man, a man claiming to be Buffalo Bill's grandson, goatee and all, was putting on a show.

Later that day I went to the judge's house and explained to him that we had to be back at school the following Monday. He was seated in a rocking chair and wearing a top hat like the one Lincoln used to wear. He ordered that Kirk be released, and we made it back to Buffalo. After the coldness of San Francisco, where we were dependent upon the hospitality of a few friends to keep us alive, I had welcomed the warmth of North Platte, Nebraska. I will never forget North Platte, Nebraska.

I BEGAN WRITING in Buffalo, New York, and in my late teens, I collaborated with some black intellectuals to build a theater group at the black YMCA, but I was getting nowhere. In 1960 I was living in the Talbert Mall projects (named for a black abolitionist) and stuck in a marriage that was destructive for my young wife, our child, and me. My main problem was that I couldn't find a job that paid a decent salary, and even though I had a few years of college, no white-collar firm would have me. I remember answering an ad for Allstate Insurance and the personnel person saying that he liked the way I sounded on the phone. He asked me to come to his suburban office for an interview. I naively thought that I had the job, even went out and bought a new suit. But when I showed up for the interview, he took one look and told me that there was nothing for me. I tried to get a job at IBM as a salesperson, but the interviewer said that my math was bad. There were no equal-opportunity or affirmative-action provisions in those days. I couldn't even get a job as a laborer at

the plant where my stepfather worked. Buffalo, a manufacturing town in those days, had been good to him and my
mother, who were part of the 1940s migration from the
South. He told me, when I announced that I was moving to
New York City, "If you can't make it in Buffalo, you can't
make it anywhere." I was stuck at a low-paying job at General
Hospital on High Street, and often I would go to the bar,
located a block away from the projects, and play "Please Mr.
Postman" by the Marvelettes. I wanted someone to deliver a
message that would get me out of my situation. I was writing
a play and acting in local theater productions, but outlets for
such expression were limited in Buffalo.

One weekend in 1962 I went to New York and hung out
at a tavern called Chumley's on Bedford Street in Greenwich
Village. On the walls, the book jackets of famous authors
who'd drank there, people like Edna St. Vincent Millay, were
on display. Hooked on the literary life, I left Buffalo for New
York in 1962. I was twenty-three years old. I joined the
Umbra workshop of African-American writers, and attended
parties where Norman Mailer, Ralph Ellison, Amiri Baraka,
and James Baldwin were holding forth. By the time I was
twenty-seven, I had a book contract with Doubleday, thanks
to the assistance of poet Langston Hughes and the late editor
Anne Freedgood.

Boxer Mike Tyson once defined *tragedy* as giving millions
of dollars to a twenty-year-old. I didn't receive even $1 mil-
lion, but I was still not ready for early literary success. I
messed up. Drank too much. Talked too much. Left a trail of
hurt feelings. I wasn't used to such attention. My poetry was

quoted in the *New York Times*. My name was dropped in gossip columns. I wasn't up to the dinners held in my honor at Doubleday's town house, the adulation of women, the fame that accompanied being young, gifted, and black in the New York of the 1960s. The jacket of my first novel, *The Free-Lance Pallbearers*, was put up on the wall at Chumley's months before the book itself had even come out.

I was living with a dancer/choreographer named Carla Blank. We had an apartment on Twenty-third Street in Chelsea. Carla was a star among an avant-garde group of dancers and artists that included Meredith Monk, Elaine Summers, and Sally Gross. Her last major public performance in New York, with collaborator Suzushi Hanayagi, titled *The Wall Street Journal*, had received a standing ovation and cheers at Judson Church. But we both felt a need for change. For new challenges.

I tell people that if I'd remained in New York, I would have been murdered by affection. Indeed New York's ability to absorb talent is one of the reasons that among American cities, it's still the most brilliant. But such affection can lull you into apathy. Alfred Kazin told Ralph Ellison that if he hadn't spent so much time hanging out at "21," Ellison could have finished his second novel, whereupon a scuffle reportedly ensued. Ellison wore out his welcome among the literati, and by the time he made a public break with his sponsors it was too late. He'd lost his creative juice. My solution to wearing out my welcome was to leave, and in 1967 Carla and I went to Los Angeles. We spent a very frugal summer there. She worked as a theater instructor at Eddie Rickenbacker's camp in the mountains. Because I had received an advance from Doubleday, I was able to remain in our apartment in Echo Park Canyon, working on my second novel, *Yellow Back Radio Broke-Down,* a deconstructionist Western, before the term became an American academic buzzword.

In September we traveled to Berkeley. We found an apartment in a ticky-tack and waited for the publication of my first novel, *The Free-Lance Pallbearers.* The book came out and nothing happened. Of course, had I remained in New York there would have been the network interviews, the parties and bookstore appearances, but I was on the West Coast, which Mike Gold, the New York communist writer of the 1930s, described as a sanatorium. I could just as soon have been in another country. We were broke, but a couple of days after I'd returned from the Berkeley unemployment office, I got a call from the late Thomas Parkinson, then professor of English at U.C. Berkeley, inviting me to teach. That was 1968. I've been teaching there ever since.

At first I lived in different Berkeley neighborhoods. I wrote *Mumbo Jumbo,* my third and best-known novel, in an apartment that was part of a huge house with a Japanese garden. It was located on Bret Harte Way, named for the famous Oaklander and chronicler of western lore. By the late seventies Carla and I were living in El Cerrito, a small, conservative town with a lot of gun shops on the main drag, located north of Berkeley. In 1979 we began house hunting in Oakland, although it had a bad reputation and I had reservations about moving there. (I had even made some unfair and disparaging remarks about the town in *The Last Days of Louisiana Red,* published in 1974.) We were about to decide upon a purchase of a house on Market Street when poet Victor Cruz's then-wife, Elisa, told us that the house we wanted was around the corner. She'd had a dream of our buying a house in Oakland and the house around the corner was a match for the one she'd seen in her dream. It was a huge Queen Anne Victorian in dilapidated condition. Having a mother whose psychic abilities are acute, I decided to take Elisa's advice. We bought it. Her wisdom has been borne out; over the years we've nearly restored the home to its original splendor.

IN 1979, when I moved to Oakland, the city was a model for black power, partially due to the efforts of the Black Panther party, which had helped to transform the city from a feudal backwater run by a few families to a modern city with worldwide recognition. From the seventies through the nineties, there was a black mayor, a black symphony conductor, a black museum head, black members of the black city council, and, in Robert Maynard, the only black publisher of a major news daily. Mayor Lionel Wilson, whom the Panthers wanted to lead a nationalist surge like Sun Yat-sen, a U.S. congressman, supervisors, and other black elected officials openly attributed their electoral success to support from the Black Panther party.

The Panthers supported the campaign of our current mayor, Jerry Brown, too, and the scene at his commune after he'd won the mayoral election in 1999 resembled a Black Panther party reunion. But soon the Panthers and many other black supporters broke with Brown. The decline of Oakland's black power began with the election of Brown, whom some say deceived his progressive black supporters with anticorporate broadcasts aired on Pacifica Radio's KPFA before the election. He wouldn't be the first Oakland mayor elected through the efforts of blacks only to abandon them once in office; a progressive conservationist mayor had done the same thing more than a hundred years earlier. The only reminder of the power that blacks once wielded might be the names of black leaders etched on downtown buildings, the post office, a courthouse, and the federal and state buildings, like monuments to now-forgotten pharaohs covered by desert sand or the Oakland schools and streets now named for forgotten invaders from New Spain (Mexico). But now that many of Brown's policies have failed, Wilson Riles Jr., the mayor's opponent in the last election, predicted that African-American influence was making a comeback, and that the mayor's much ballyhooed plan to draw middle-income blacks and hi-techers at the expense of low-income blacks would fail. A couple of days after interviewing Wilson Riles Jr. for this book, my daughter Tennessee and I ran into Dori Maynard, daughter of the late Robert Maynard, at DeLauer's, Oakland's all-night newsstand. As if to confirm Riles's comment about a black comeback, Dori said that she and some other black Oaklanders were restoring a Victorian block in West Oakland under a first-time home ownership plan, planting roots.

Still, as a result of Brown's "elegant density" plan announced during his 1999 campaign—nicknamed "10K" because it aimed to bring ten thousand new residents into downtown Oakland—many poor residents and residents of modest means are finding themselves priced out of the city. Brown had promised that this wouldn't happen. He described his elegant density plan in a speech that was reprinted in a 1999 article in *Whole Earth* magazine: "He wants to create construction jobs and stimulate the retail and entertainment sectors. He's trying to bring 10,000 people to live downtown. He's trying not to overwhelm these areas with too much new traffic or turn downtown Oakland into a gentrified hub at the expense of low-income residents."

To provide a model city for elegant density, Brown invoked Manhattan.

I'm trying to do things that will, at least indirectly, deal with the issue of sustainability. That's why I've said, Let's have some density. Instead of a vision of Pleasanton [a local suburb], we could have a vision of Manhattan. In fact, at one meeting, I said, Think Hong Kong. That's come back to me with derision. People don't like that, because they like space. So I've tried to create an image that would make it more acceptable. I call it "elegant density." Have you ever tried to go from one side of Manhattan to another? That's "elegant density." People are close to one another. You have time in your car. You're not going to get there in five minutes, so you can enjoy having a conversation with the person with you.

You have to enjoy where you are. It is a lot of people and it is alive and there is culture and art, and yes, there is money and investment. It's a hell of a civilization. I don't know how sustainable it is, but it is active.

Brown's use of Manhattan as a model should have been the tip-off, because black and Puerto Rican removal has been the policy of several recent New York mayors. Moreover, none of us who supported Brown had heeded the warning from the *San Francisco Bay View*, a black newspaper, which noticed how the Brown campaign staff included few minorities.

Eviction rates have tripled since he took office. Three-quarters of these evictions have been reported by African-Americans, Latinos, and Asian-Americans. Rents have increased 20 to 30 percent in the last three years. For some, the invasion of the hi-techers, the '99ers, from San Francisco and elsewhere, can be regarded as the worst disaster to happen to Oakland since the invasion of the '49ers, the gold-crazed hordes who came crashing into Oakland in the mid-1800s. Classical buildings and traditional landmarks are being leveled and replaced by vertical trailer parks that seem to go up overnight. The success of Brown's operation hinged upon the continuation of a booming hi-tech economy. Why, with his New Age Zen smarts, Brown couldn't foresee the bubble's bursting is puzzling. The signs were visible in 1999. Now, because of Brown's blindness, the ugly boxlike condominiums are vacant in a slumping market, according to a powerful Realtor. Brown is not the first Oakland mayor to be swallowed by the downtown Brasília fantasy.

When Mayor Brown was asked whether his plan to gen-
trify downtown would threaten diversity, he replied ("tartly,"
according to his supporter George Will), "There is no diversity there now. You have a concentrated, homogenous population—the elderly, parolees, people in rehab, from mental
hospitals, transients. This is not the vibrant civic culture
some might have in mind." Obviously, this is not the Brown
who worked alongside Mother Teresa.

Having observed the fine work of Sisters Caroline and
Maureen at Friendly Manor, a halfway house for women in
recovery located on San Pablo in downtown Oakland, I
thought this remark especially cruel. I contrasted it with
remarks that 1900 mayoral candidate Jack London, a socialist, made before a gathering of wealthy New Yorkers: "You
have been entrusted with the world; you have muddled and
mismanaged it. You are incompetent, despite all your boast-
ings. A million years ago the caveman, without tools, with
small brain, and with nothing but the strength of his body,
managed to feed his wife and children, so that through him
the race survived. You, on the other hand, armed with all
the modern means of production, multiplying the produc-
tive capacity of the caveman a million times—you incom-
petents and muddlers, you are unable to secure to millions
even the paltry amount of bread that would sustain their
physical life. You have mismanaged the world and it shall be
taken from you!" Having been born out of wedlock and
having lived in poverty during his childhood, Jack London,
were he alive today, would probably be part of that "concentrated, homogenous population" at which Brown aimed

his Marie Antoinette–like sneer. Clearly, there would have been no place for Jack London in Jerry Brown's Oakland. London said, "I had been born poor. Poor I had lived. I had gone hungry on occasion. I had never had toys nor [sic] playthings like other children. My first memories of life were pinched by poverty. The pinch of poverty had been chronic."

IN THE LATE AFTERNOON downtown Oakland still resembles the blue-collar Canal Street of New Orleans more than it does Fifth Avenue. The dot-commers, hi-techers, siliconers, and others who were summoned to Oakland when Brown announced his elegant density plan in 1999 wouldn't be the first invasion to change the face of the city. The new '99ers, like their forebears in the 1849 Gold Rush, chose not to abide by the Calvinist ethic and accumulate wealth over the long haul but chose to get rich quick. They have that in common with the gang members—outlaw capitalists—who were responsible for Oakland's high murder rate in 2002, the 150th anniversary of the city's founding by men who might today be called white-collar criminals. These founders leased land from a member of a Mexican family, then violated the lease by selling it to squatters. By the time the courts sided with the Peralta family, the squatters had established a city with the lead swindler electing himself mayor. Clearly crime waves are nothing new to Oakland.

Homelessness isn't new to California, either. By boat, the '49ers embarked from San Francisco for Oakland. From there they traveled to the Sierra foothills, the site of gold's discovery. Instead of uprooting African-Americans, Latinos, and Asian-Americans, as the '99ers are doing, the gold rushers drove out the New Spanish and the Native American populations through genocide and land theft. One witness says that the invaders treated the Indians as though they were wild animals. From the beginning of the Gold Rush to its end, the Native American population was reduced from about three hundred thousand to twenty-six thousand. But just as the bubble of the dot-com rush burst, so did that of the '49ers. Bret Harte, who was run out of Humboldt County for complaining about the Gunther Island Massacre of Indian women and children in 1860, writes about visiting mining camps and finding the once-hopeful miners destitute. (Bret Harte's neighborhood is remembered by some Victorian houses located at 567–577 Fifth Street, which is called Bret Harte Boardwalk Historic District.) After the craze for gold ended, the miners, according to historian Mary Jo Wainwright, came out of the mountains looking for land. The New Spanish had the land, which the American invaders from the east began squatting on or, as in the case of the original Oakland squatters, obtaining through lengthy court battles that were deliberately prolonged so that by the time the courts decided in favor of the new Spanish, ownership of the land became a moot point.

The gold rushers arrived at the foot of Broadway, where the American occupation of California's interior begins. It is called Jack London Square, and a bronze statue of the author stands before the Oakland estuary, once called the Contra Costa Bayou. (Contra Costa means "other shore.") California has never recovered from the damage caused by those earlier invaders, the '49ers, and their treatment of the California natives must rank as one of the cruelest episodes in human history. Moreover, tons of mercury used in processing the gold are still poisoning the wildlife of the bay. Whether Oakland will recover from the invasion of the '99ers remains to be seen.

BROWN'S TOUGH-LOVE posture towards blacks and the poor has earned him an award from the far-right Manhattan Institute and kudos from white supremacist columnist George Will. But shortly after the endorsements, Brown made a stirring anticapitalist speech, which only increased his reputation for flakiness. Blacks are moving east to the Sacramento Valley and elsewhere, where living costs are more reasonable. Oakland, however, hasn't become New Hampshire yet. And so, even with the black drain that is occurring under Brown, Oakland still hosts one of the most ethnically diverse populations in the country, a callaloo of cultures. In the winter of 2001, in preparation for writing this book, I attended a black cowboy parade, a Kwanzaa celebration, and a powwow. In addition, I visited Yoshi's, Oakland's landmark nightclub located in Jack London Square, and heard a Lakota musician play John Coltrane's "Naima" in traditional Lakota style. Oakland is a city where identities blur. Where one encounters hip-hop dancers at a festival in Chinatown; where the mistress of ceremonies at a Kwanzaa celebration is a white woman in Yoruba dress; where, perhaps less surprising, about a fifth of the audience at a Native American powwow is black. As if those events weren't enough to reflect the cultural stew, I attended a springtime carnival that celebrated Oshun, a Nigerian "saint." Oshun, daughter of the Yoruba god Olodumare, who made the crossing to Brazil when blacks first arrived there, has become a fashion inspiration to black women in Oakland and elsewhere. (This wouldn't be the only Oakland event I attended during the 150th anniversary of the city at which African "saints" were invoked—Milton Cardona, who appears on a record called *Conjure,* which features my songs and poetry, invoked Elegba during a performance on drums at Yoshi's while accompanying Don Byron, known for mixing jazz with klezmer music.) On August 24, 2002, I went to the Chinatown fest and watched Polynesian dancers perform under the watchful eye of a dark-skinned biracial leader named Mahea. Despite the failure of arts middlepersons to serve Oakland's artistic community, writing this book has convinced me that among American cities, Oakland is unique. It combines the beauty of the West, the mountains, rivers, and forests, with the gritty naturalism of old northeastern industrial towns. When you watch the crowds of blacks, Asians, and Hispanics coexisting peacefully in the late afternoon on Broadway and Fourteenth, near the Tribune Tower, you get a glimpse of what the world could look like.

But of all of the events I attended in connection with the

writing of this book, those that drew the biggest audiences
were those in which the legendary Oakland blues singers
sang, preached, and shouted out the blues. Oakland is Blues
City, and one of the reasons I like it here is because it has
the feel of labor cities in the Northeast such as Detroit,
Cleveland, and Buffalo. Oakland is Buffalo with weather.
Husky and brawling like Carl Sandburg's "Chicago"—and
not like one of Sandburg's "soft cities" that the current
administration desires Oakland to become, or like San
Francisco, poet George Sterling's "Cool, Grey City of Love."
The difference between Mayor Brown and some of us is
more than political. There are aesthetic differences as well.
Blues is the music of the working class, of the brawling and
husky, and one of the nation's largest blues festivals, drawing
as many as forty thousand people, is the Annual BBQ, Blues,
and Beer Festival. It takes place each year near next door to
Everett and Jones Barbecue, located in Jack London Square.
I was standing near a fence, dancing in place, taking photos
and notes, when Jerry Brown showed up. Nobody noticed
him. He looked lost. The blues people complain that they
don't receive as much support from the city as the gay pride
parade does. The Black Cowboys make the same complaint.
But if Brown wants to do a makeover of Oakland, which for
some is still the ugly stepsister of San Francisco, the stepsister
is resisting. Oakland has more in common with Bret Harte's
Cherokee Sal than with Jeanette McDonald. More in common with the blues than with soft rock.

The Birthplace of Oakland

A T 10:00 A.M. my daughter Tennessee and I show up for the Jack London waterfront walking tour, sponsored by the city of Oakland. There are five of us, including an African-American author whose reason for being there is an interest in things Oakland. He says he's shown up for some of my poetry readings. I apologize for boring him. There's an elderly white couple from Barthrup-on-Humber, an English town that boasts a church almost a thousand years old. They are dressed for gardening. The tour begins at 101 Broadway, the location of the old Overland House restaurant built in 1887 and now home to Barclay's Restaurant. Our tour guides, two relaxed senior citizens named Virginia La Faille and Pearl McCurthy, are dressed casually in golf hats, patterned blouses, and black pants. We head toward the foot of Broadway, which originated as an Indian dirt path, then became a cattle trail, and then a streetcar line connecting

Oakland and Berkeley. This is where the American history of Oakland begins. Moses Chase, a Yankee settler, landed here in 1849 and set up a tent on land belonging to Luis Maria Peralta. A conniving wheeler-dealer named Horace W. Carpentier (born Carpenter), Oakland's first mayor, obtained sole ownership of the entire waterfront in 1852, as a result of double-dealing the Peralta family.

We visit the port of Oakland, the third-largest port on the West Coast and the fourth largest in the United States. The *Cielo D. Europa Cagliari* is in the port today and the cranes, some of which are twenty stories high, unload its cargo onto the dock. Oakland was the first major port on the West Coast to build terminals for what port literature describes as "then-revolutionary containerships, becoming the second largest port in the world in container tonnage in the late 1960s and second only to New York in container terminal acreage." The goods carried by the container ships, thirty to forty of which pass through the port daily, are loaded and unloaded for distribution throughout the world.

The importance of the port would hit home during the last week of September 2002, when the longshoremen would go on strike over the issues of safety and the union's quest to control jobs tied to new technology. Thousands of pounds of vegetables meant for Asia would lie rotting on the dock. Auto parts, furniture, shoes, and toys would remain unloaded. More than 60 percent of the country's computer equipment passes through the port. Without the port, retailers would have to pay for expensive airfreight, which costs three times as much as shipping, and pass the costs on to consumers. The longshoreman's strike would total losses of $1 billion for each day of the strike, a refreshing reminder that the roots of the city and the country are in sweaty labor, and testimony to the power of blue-collar muscle-flexing.

Ferries that run round-trip to San Francisco are also located here at the foot of Broadway. These ferries came in handy after the 1989 Loma Prieta earthquake damaged some of the East Bay's freeways. Captain Thomas Gray, grandfather of famous dancer Isadora Duncan, began the first ferry service to San Francisco in 1850. The USS *Potomac,* a yacht that once belonged to Franklin Roosevelt, is docked at the ferry terminal. Built in 1934 as the Coast Guard cutter *Electra,* it became a presidential yacht in 1936. Called the "floating White House" by Eleanor Roosevelt, it is the prize of the waterfront. Among those whom the president entertained on the yacht were King George VI and Queen Elizabeth. One of the tour guides says that for $75 you can book a luncheon on the yacht and take an excursion on the water. The booking office is nearby. Five million dollars, mostly Oakland money, was raised to restore the yacht, which had fallen into disrepair as well as ill repute. At one time, it was in the possession of drug dealers. When the U.S. Customs Office auctioned it off the port of Oakland was the only bidder. It went for $15,000.

Around the corner from the booking office, which displays photos from the time when the *Potomac* was more than an exhibition ship, sits Yoshi's, one of the most famous jazz clubs in the world. Formerly located on Claremont Street in Berkeley, it was lured to its present site by a subsidy from the

ISHMAEL REED

city of Oakland. We pass Jack London Cinema, one of the
new-style multiplexes with reclining seats with cups for
drinks, en route to a building that was once Oakland's
Western Pacific Railroad Station. It was saved from demolition in 1974 by Oakland's city planning department and
named Oakland's number one landmark. At one time, Oakland's port was controlled by a Central (later Southern) Pacific
Railroad subsidiary that had been formed by one of San
Francisco's big four: Charles Crocker, Collis P. Huntington,
Mark Hopkins, and Leland Stanford. Rebecca Solnit, author
of *River of Shadows,* says of the big four, "Their corruption
was as vast as their profit!" According to Abby Wasserman in
her anthology, *The Spirit of Oakland,* the agreement to bring
the railroad to Oakland was actually brokered by Dr. Samuel
Merritt, the city's mayor in 1868. The first mayor, Horace W.
Carpentier, ran the waterfront and the railroads through
scheming and conniving until the 1900s, when he was chal-
lenged by Jay Gould. The passenger station opened in 1910.
In the 1940s kings, movie stars, and presidents, along with
thousands of other passengers, boarded the legendary
Zephyr, a diesel-powered streamliner with a Vistadome roof
that one could take from Oakland to Chicago. The original
Zephyr was discontinued in 1970. When the Oakland station
became the terminus for the West Coast, winning out over
San Francisco, Oakland began to grow from a suburb of San
Francisco and a resort town for rich San Franciscans to a city
with a burgeoning population of its own.

Our journey continues past Kimball's Carnival, a Latin
dance club that boasts eighteen billiard tables and salsa lessons

on Wednesdays. If you like the blues, Bluesville, a blues club, is located nearby. We pass eating places such as The Bistro Cafe, The Fat Lady, Everett and Jones Barbecue, and the Oakland Grill, where the mayor has breakfast from time to time. Then we reach the produce area. Truckloads of vegetables and fruit are brought here from the Central Valley farmland to be bought by Oakland restaurants. These produce warehouses used to be run by the Italians, who once lived in this district. They've been replaced by Cambodians, Laotians, and Vietnamese. In the old days, industries settled near Jack London Square to be near the railroads, but most of them have given way to live/work lofts, apartments, and condominiums built for the new arrivals, the '99ers. To remind us of the past, signs on building walls read THE AMERICAN BAG COMPANY or ALLIED PAPER CO., but just for show, to lend a texture of grit so the newcomers can enjoy their authentic surroundings. A new postmodern version of the old station is located near the mayor's commune-style residence, which has the ironic name of "We the People." As a fully credentialed Boho, Jerry Brown maintains a countercultural style while practicing a brutal capitalist philosophy. A group of cowboy policemen, called the "riders," on trial for terrorizing young African-American men, said in their defense that they thought they were carrying out the mayor's mandate.

This new train station was named for C. L. Dellums, and includes some of the wooden benches from the old station. In the first half of the twentieth century, the railroads brought thousands of blacks to Oakland. C. L. Dellums was one of them. An African-American from Corsicana, Texas, he began work as a Pullman car porter in 1924. In 1925 he was elected West Coast vice president of the Brotherhood of Sleeping Car Porters, which at the time was led by its first president, A. Philip Randolph. The brotherhood was the first black union chartered by the AFL, and the job of a porter, while still a kind of domestic, was among the best available to black men in the years before the civil rights movement. The union also became known for its social activism beyond the world of train porters. For many years, Dellums tackled such issues as police brutality and the miserable conditions in which black agricultural workers existed. In 1968, Dellums succeeded Randolph as president of the Brotherhood of Sleeping Car Porters. The new train station, then, serves as another concrete reminder of Oakland's roots in labor and resistance, roots that have withstood waves of urban crisis and gentrification so far. C. L. Dellums's nephew, Congressman Ronald Dellums, served the Berkeley-Oakland district for many years, and the recently built twin-towered federal building is named for him.

Crossing the sky bridge connecting the station to the site of what was once Jack London Village affords an excellent view of Jack London Square and the surrounding area. We pass an empty lot, slated to become a parking lot for '99ers dwelling in a new development with the generic name "The Landing," and head toward a wooden shack. It's the famous Heinold's First and Last Chance Saloon at the foot of Webster Street, and we find it in the same condition as when it was built in 1880 from the timber of old ships. East Bay Bohemian writers Bret Harte, Rex Beach, Robert

Louis Stevenson, Joaquin Miller, and Jack London drank here. John Heinold came to San Francisco from Philadelphia in 1876 and bought the bunkhouse for $100. Its original purpose was to serve as a bunkhouse for men who worked in the oyster beds. On June 1, 1883, though, Heinold opened the First and Last Chance Saloon, calling it that because for sailors, it was their first chance to have a drink on coming ashore and last chance on shipping out. Sailors often left bills on the wall for good luck, to reclaim when they came back safely—although many never made it back from their dangerous labor. Jack London, who hung around picking up sailing stories, mentions the First and Last Chance Saloon seventeen times in his autobiographical work, *John Barleycorn*.

A stone's throw from the shack is Scott's Restaurant, formerly called The Sea Wolf after another of London's books. One of my favorite places in the city, Scott's features seafood, and a jazz group led by a mellow pianist performs here. You can go out to the patio and catch an excellent view of the estuary and the port, water, ships, and seamen.

Not too far from Heinold's First and Last Chance Saloon sits the cabin where London lived during the Yukon gold rush, which was moved to Oakland in 1970. Our tour ends here. From Jack London Square, the city of Oakland began to creep uptown toward what is now called Old Oakland. The squatters who "founded" the town, Horace W. Carpentier, Edson Adams, and Andrew J. Moon, hired a Swiss engineer, Julius Kellersberger, to map out streets in their three adjacent holdings in the grid pattern typical of all nineteenth-century towns in the United States. Streets were numbered or named after presidents. Alice Street, the location of the Alice Arts Center, was named for Carpentier's sister. The Alice Arts Center was in the news during the time of our tour because the Brown administration had threatened to evict some African-American arts groups from the center in order to make way for an elite arts academy, 35 percent of whose students were to be drawn from out of town, despite the abundance of homegrown talent generously displayed at every event I attended during this anniversary year for the city. Authenticity can't be too real.

AUGUST 21

Today's our day for touring Old Oakland. The boundaries of Old Oakland are Tenth and Seventh Streets, Broadway and Clay. Jack London said that taverns dominated the businesses between Tenth and Seventh on Broadway in the old days, not a surprising observation, especially coming from London. We meet our tour guide, Betty Marvin, whose appearance is that of someone dressed for the stacks. Someone who does not let up until the last footnote yields, but not necessarily someone Jack London would've run into in the taverns of the old city. The Old Oakland walk begins in front of a building located at 825 Washington Street in Oakland's first commercial district, built in response to the arrival of the railroads. A. J. Gooch erected the building, called a "block" in the old days, where our group meets. In 1876 Gooch was identified in a city directory with "capitalist" as his occupation. The building began as the Windsor Hotel, but has gone through transformations since then. Its architecture is Italianate, a style popular in the 1870s. As thousands of people arrived in Oakland to work on the railroads, they settled in West Oakland, whose houses were built in the same Italianate, or Italianate Villa, style: low, pitched roofs; L- or U-shaped windows; a few stories tall. As in most cities, one can identify the dates during which Oakland buildings were built by style. Oakland architects of the 1880s preferred the Stick style, while the Victorian style was popular during the 1890s.

When the center of commerce moved further uptown in the early twentieth century and modernism became the vogue, not only in architecture but in the arts, Old Oakland, or Victorian row, became skid row. After touring the Oakland homes occupied by the rich in the Victorian era, one can argue that wealthy people such as poet Amy Lowell who could afford grand tours to collect culture from all over the world provided the impetus for modernism.

By combining the old and the new, postmodernists fashioned new gargoyles from fiberglass because the wooden ones were infected with dry rot, and beginning in 1982, Old Oakland was renovated with funds from the City of Oakland Redevelopment Agency. With the aim of bringing back some of the features that had been lost when Old Oakland was neglected, architects did some touching up: A cornice that was missing from A. J. Gooch's building was restored, as were the bay windows on the Leimert building, located at 456 Eighth Street, which had previously been sacrificed in favor of the flat modern look. The Storek brothers, Glen and Richard, who directed the renovation of Old Oakland, consulted old library photographs in order to give the Oakland buildings their original look. The past is never lost completely; rediscovery is always possible.

Among the stores and restaurants on the block where we meet are Ratto's grocery, which has been operated by the same family since 1896, and the Old Oakland Hotel. Another piece of nineteenth-century history on this stretch is the Oakland Free Market, which was part of the city's burgeoning commercial district in the 1870s. At this site, later known as the Housewives' Market, independent vendors were allowed to sell their wares from stalls. Its building occupies a whole city block and is one of Old Oakland's most interesting, with its terra-cotta facade featuring sculptures of fruit, vegetables, and livestock. These scenes appear on City Hall as well. We are told by our guide that the fruit was supposed to symbolize California's abundance, the perpetual promised land of the West. Nothing communicates the contrast between old-style architecture and modernism more than the charming old railroad station on Seventh Street, with its nooks and crannies and detailed facade. Across the street is the Bauhaus-style police station, icy and distant.

AUGUST 28

Tennessee and I show up for the City Center tour. Our guide today is Renate Coombs, a redheaded, freckled-faced, middle-aged woman who, like the two swinging seniors who led us on the Jack London waterfront tour, is dressed casually—Renate wears white sneakers, socks, jeans, and a T-shirt featuring pictures of penguins. There are about five other people on this tour. We're standing in front of Oakland's fifth City Hall, built between 1911 and 1914 and reputed to be the first high-rise City Hall west of the Mississippi. Part of the exhibit inside City Hall includes photos of city halls built prior to the present one. Two were storefronts. The first was located on Broadway and Third Streets. The second, on Broadway and Eighth. There's a sign on the second City Hall that announces AN OPEN FORUM EVERY SUNDAY NIGHT. At that time, Renate tells me, white men ruled the town, as they would for much of the city's history and as they do now. A third City Hall was built and burned in 1877. It was replaced by a fourth City Hall, which stood in front of the current one.

Inside, attached to the ceiling above the top of an ornate staircase, hangs a light fixture containing 128 bulbs. It's called a disco ball by the irreverent. It's been part of the building since 1914, when City Hall opened. The ball was added to show off electricity and to represent the dawning of the twentieth century. The bronze rings encircling the ball show figures designed to represent the planets. This City Hall at one time housed the fire station and the jail; behind the ornate clock tower that stands at the top of City Hall, the narrow windows of the onetime jail can be seen. In the old days, children were advised that they'd be "put behind the clock" if they didn't behave. The clock is anchored by four posts. It was within ten seconds of falling from its perch atop

City Hall during the 1989 earthquake because three of the posts holding it up were destroyed. The last post, seconds from toppling, held when the earth stopped shaking.

After City Hall was damaged by the earthquake, some English engineers were consulted about shielding the building from future earthquake damage, and it was renovated so that now it doesn't touch the earth but rests on shock absorbers and is surrounded by a moat. Prior to the election of Jerry Brown, Oakland mayors presided over council meetings where they often engaged in testy exchanges with the public and council members. After the election of Brown, a "strong mayor" measure was passed; since then, a council member told me, Brown's relationship with the council has been cool. An imperial mayor, he's surrounded by those whom a local gadfly columnist refers to as "Brownies." People who know what is best for Oakland, if only Oaklanders would move out of the way.

AUGUST 30

Today Carla and I drive to a location known as the birthplace of Oakland. We arrive at a site that features a house of Victorian Italianate style. This is the Peralta House, named for the family headed by Luis Maria Peralta, who in 1820, at the age of sixty-two, received forty-five thousand acres from Pablo de Sola, the last Spanish governor of Alta California, in recognition of service to the Spanish crown. Peralta had arrived in California at the age of sixteen as part of an

exploratory expedition led by Juan Bautista de Anza and hung
around until his death. The Peralta grant included present-day
Oakland, Berkeley, Albany, El Cerrito, Emeryville, Piedmont,
and part of San Leandro.

After being neglected for generations, perhaps as a way of
ignoring the shameful chapter of the city's history that it
represents, the Peralta House is being restored and is slated to
become a museum. The house reminds us that the first
mayor of Oakland, Horace W. Carpentier, and his cronies
were thieves. In her book *Oakland: The Story of a City,* Beth
Bagwell gives these men the benefit of the doubt when, in a
footnote, she writes, "Historians still dispute whether the
three [Carpentier, Edson Adams, and Andrew J. Moon]
deliberately defrauded the Peraltas or whether they believed,
like many others at the time, that U.S. sovereignty super-
seded Mexican claims and opened the way for legitimate
claims by American citizens on public land." This is a strange
argument, given that a number of U.S. court decisions sided
with the Peraltas against the squatters.

In her book *The Spirit of Oakland,* Abby Wasserman
paints a far more sinister portrait of Carpentier, a twenty-
six-year-old New Yorker and graduate in law of Columbia
University: "He made an early career of wrestling Peralta
land from the family, acting alternately as counselor and con-
fiscator. He is rumored to have dressed as a priest and performed bogus rituals at the Peralta rancho. He was also
accused of rustling cattle, filing exhaustive and endless
appeals, claims, and litigation, and keeping courts, cohorts,

and correspondents at arm's length for years." A living descendant of the Peraltas is more blunt, saying that her ancestors were swindled and, after the squatters had occupied much of their property, persecuted, pushed off their lands, and reduced to poverty. Historian Mary Jo Wainwright, who wrote her dissertation on the Peraltas, agrees. She says that Vicente Peralta, whose father, Luis, left him what is now Old Oakland and downtown Oakland, was swindled of his birthright by the cunning New Yorker.

Carla and I are greeted at a tall, ornate door of the Peralta House by Grey Kolevzon, a young redheaded man in a T-shirt and jeans. He is barefoot. Three black children are playing inside while three young white women, the staff, are at work. Kolevzon gives us a cursory tour of the house and directs us to Wainwright, who, luckily for us, is on her way to Oakland to tell the history of the Peraltas on a tour of famous Oakland houses. Wainwright agrees to meet Carla and me at 3:00 P.M. at the end of her official tour.

We arrive at the park to see tourists departing from the hacienda. They are senior citizens, mostly, and enjoying themselves. They praise the box lunch: cheese, pasta, salad, and soda water. Though Wainwright has been talking to this group for an hour, she has enough enthusiasm for the Peraltas and their legacy to lead us through their history for an additional hour and a half.

Oakland is celebrating its 150th anniversary, dating from its founding by Carpentier, the man who "swindled" the Peraltas out of their land, but the actual European history of Oakland begins on this site. Indeed, the Peraltas are Oakland's first European family. Up until the Peraltas' arrival, Spanish soldiers had so abused Native American women that a decision was made to send soldiers' wives and children along with them to what is now Oakland. (Rather than give birth to children born as a result of rape by those whom they considered their oppressors, the Indian women chose abortion and infanticide.)

Peralta and his wife, Maria Loreto Alviso Peralta, who had seventeen children of their own, arrived in California with the De Anza expedition. Two of his sons built the Oakland adobe in 1821. Often described as short and black, Peralta may have had African heritage. He complained that suitors were attracted to one of his daughters because of her money not her beauty. He said that she was too dark. When the Americans arrived, they found a mixed-race population; some of the Afro-Mexicans had come from the same state in Mexico as the Peraltas. Perhaps the Peraltas were the first victims of black removal! Holly Alonso, the director of Friends of the Peralta Hacienda, tells us that before the miscegenephobic Americans came, racism was absent from California culture; indeed, many of the new arrivals who established a white supremacist standard in California were Celtic-Americans who, ironically, weren't considered "white" in the eastern United States. But before the arrival of the Americans, the population here was mixed Native American, European, and African. As a testimony to this fact, a display at the hacienda features a photo of a white man and his Native American wife.

The Peraltas' first home, an adobe, was built in 1821.

It was replaced by other adobes, guest houses, and work buildings, which all became part of the two-and-a-half-acre hacienda. For his service, which included rounding up fugitive Indians and returning them to missions where they were used as slave labor and prostitutes, Peralta was granted this spread. Down the hill from the house lies a creek, which, according to Mary Jo, is one of the reasons the Peraltas chose this site on which to build. The Peralta land was worked by Indians who had left the missions; one of these was an Indio named José Guzmán, who recorded eleven songs in his native language, some of the earliest such recordings.

Along our tour we hear two explanations as to why Indians had Spanish names (such as Guzmán). One was that the Spanish gave them the names; the other that Indians took Spanish names to avoid extermination, which was one of the solutions to the Indian problem in California. In January 1851, Governor Burnett delivered a message to the new California legislature: "A war of extermination will continue to be waged between the two races, until the Indian race becomes extinct. . . . While we cannot anticipate this result with but painful regret, the inevitable destiny of the race is beyond the power and wisdom of man to avert."

Preservation Park and the
Jewel of Oakland

JUNE 11

I T'S SPRINGTIME IN Oakland, and Denise Lewis is cool
and poised. She sits comfortably in a chair on the second
floor of the Preservation Park building in which she works
as part of the park's administrative staff. Downstairs a
Brazilian restaurant specializes in a dish of beans, rice, and
sausage. Later today the city council will decide whether
to sell Preservation Park to the East Bay Community
Foundation.

Located in downtown Oakland, Preservation Park was
once one of the city's main residential areas before downtown
became industrial. Over the years, the park's sixteen turn-of-
the-century Victorian buildings have been renovated—
facades restored and surroundings transformed into carefully
tended lawns and gardens, with other Victorian touches, such

as park benches and street lamps, added—to house offices. Restoring Preservation Park cost the city $11 million, which included the cost of relocating historic buildings from other parts of the city. The council is considering selling it for $6.5 million. The park has been making money for the city, but someone higher up, possibly the mayor, who, some say, won't be satisfied until he privatizes all of Oakland, thinks selling it is a good idea. The announcement that it might be sold has mobilized the tenants, who, after holding a number of meetings, decided to favor one bidder, the East Bay Community Foundation. Denise Lewis doesn't know whether the potential new owners will keep her on.

Denise has been working since the age of sixteen. She grew up in San Francisco's Bayview Hunter's Point, a black section of town where social and environmental toxins are rampant, and attended Telton and Balboa high schools. She worked mostly for businesses and law firms, she says, until she was recruited to work for Bramalea, the company that developed Oakland City Center, of which Preservation Park is a part. Preservation Park was the idea of developer Glen Isaacson, whose notion was to attract tenants by offering housing for nonprofits. (The Before Columbus Foundation, of which I am a director, has its office there.) Denise obtained a real estate license and handled all of the construction contracts for relocating a set of endangered historic houses that were brought to Preservation Park for renovation.

At first, Preservation Park was considered no-man's-land. An outpost. Getting tenants was hard. Though the real estate community thought leasing or renting space to nonprofits unwise, Denise says that the nonprofits pay their rent on time, an unexpected plus.

Eleven years later, Preservation Park hums with activity. It contains forty-seven tenants. According to Denise, tenant-management relationships are very good. Five of the sixteen Victorian houses, including the Nile and Ginn houses, were already located there, while others were brought from else-where in the city. Some had been slated for demolition.

Denise's first job at Preservation Park was the Oakland Festival of the Lake, an event that drew thousands of Oaklanders until a police riot closed it down. Denise and Susanne, her former boss who has since retired, had man-aged to draw in all segments of the community to the festi-val, low-riders as well as rappers, hills residents as well as flatlanders. Susanne and Denise also spent some of their work hours fighting off those who wanted to turn this non-profit island of elegance into another casualty of hyperde-velopment. Denise reports that Susanne is enjoying her retirement and has just visited the Galápagos, where the Darwinian struggle for survival is probably less intense than that found in Oakland.

SEPTEMBER 17

I attend the picnic at Preservation Park for all of the park's nonprofit tenants, not only to hear the latest on the decision to sell this historic park, but to sample the cuisine, which, under the direction of Susanne and her successor, Denise, has always been a feast. Today is no different. It is another beautiful day in Oakland. Some say that Oakland has the best weather in the United States, and I believe it. The sky is as Auburn poet Clark Ashton Smith perfectly described it: "lotus blue." We sit at tables underneath umbrellas while Ted Lacey, who manages the park for CMP Asset Managers, addresses the nonprofit representatives whose offices are housed in the historic buildings. Lacey thanks the tenants for calling the city and supporting the management of the park. He says that the pending sale of the park has been put off indefinitely. Perhaps this victory for the preservationists has been won because someone in city hall realized that even with nonprofits, Preservation Park is making a profit while some of the city's privately run redevelopment projects have collapsed.

SEPTEMBER 25

Tennessee is working at her teaching job at the New Age Academy. It's a private school founded by Gloria Cooper, an energetic black teacher who adheres to a rugged back-to-basics curriculum. They're covering Homer's *Odyssey,* a book that would be slammed by contemporary critics for its weighted-down plot and extraneous details about bull sacrifices, which seem to be excuses for partying. I am reading this magnificent book again and wonder why it isn't classified with the Koran or the Bible as a book of religion. Wrong religion, I guess. Also, what contemporary writer would get away with introducing gods and goddesses to move the plot when stuck?

So today I'm touring solo. The tour meets in front of the
Paramount Theatre. There's a young couple—a white man
and an Asian woman—on board. They live on Fifteenth
Street near Lake Merritt, a neighborhood dubbed the Gold
Coast because of its proximity to Oakland's jewel. There are
luxury apartments being constructed there, one of which
goes by the ridiculously pretentious name "Essex." This
building was hardly occupied when a dispute occurred
between the landlord and an organization called CALM,
Coalition of Advocates for Lake Merritt, which objected to a
banner erected over ten stories of the building's facade, adver-
tising the apartments. Naomi Schiff of Oakland Heritage
Alliance found the building's lighted tower even more offen-
sive, according to the *Oakland Tribune*. "What's really horrible
is that light on top; it's disgusting, the worst kind of light pollution," she said. In Oakland things like "light pollution" still
matter, at least to some folks. Buildings like the Essex are rising all over Oakland as a result of the mayor's 10K plan, a
trend vigorously opposed by some members of the heritage
and preservation lobbies, who accuse the Boho mayor of
being "development hungry." Film director Francis Ford
Coppola set up a site at the Old Oakland Hotel, built in 1915
on the Gold Coast, to shoot his film *Tucker*. He said that the
Gold Coast area reminded him of the California of the forties and fifties. Our guide, Annalee Allen, explains that this
district gives that impression because many of the buildings
were built in the twenties and thirties. In the twenties the
Victorian houses around Lake Merritt were either subdivided
or replaced by high-rises.

The area where the Paramount stands was once rural. The downtown of the late 1880s began at the foot of Broadway, the location of Jack London Square, and ended at Fourteenth Street, which included much of what is now called Old Oakland. After the famous 1906 earthquake, two hundred thousand people arrived in Oakland from San Francisco, an invasion of refugees that increased the population and required new services, retail stores, and other enterprises. In 1930 the Paramount, an Art Deco movie palace designed by architect Timothy Pflueger, was built, capturing the spirit of Jazz Age design. One feature of its elaborate design is a facade composed of twelve thousand terra-cotta tiles, creating the image of a giant puppeteer manipulating the various acts that appeared there over the years. The Paramount reached its zenith in the 1940s, when prosperity, fostered by the war, allowed many to flock downtown to films and dances and live music. In the 1950s, with the advent of television, attendance at the theater fell off, and by the early 1970s the Paramount had been abandoned. Later that decade, however, the Paramount was restored with $1 million in redevelopment funds and became a city, state, and national historic landmark. Simultaneously, the building of freeways and the Caldecott Tunnel moved the action from downtown to the suburbs.

But the glorious architecture of the modernist moment still stands in downtown Oakland, and in more buildings than one. One of the families affected by the earthquake disaster was that of Isaac Magnin. His wife, a lace maker who specialized in making undergarments for women of the carriage trade, was the mastermind behind the I. Magnin store, a branch of which stood at Twentieth and Broadway and is built in the Art Deco style. Its architects also built the Mark Hopkins Hotel, made famous in Alfred Hitchcock's film *Vertigo*.

To the west of I. Magnin is Sears, which was once H. C. Capwells and later Emporium Capwells, a department store built by the Capwells, who came from the East. The Capwells store was designed by the same architect who designed New York's Lord and Taylor and Bloomingdales. Emporium Capwell suffered damage during the 1989 earthquake. Sears has moved into the building while the former Sears store, located on Telegraph Avenue, is being converted into work loft space that will benefit the 10Kers. Having moved from his commune in Jack London Square, Mayor Brown now resides here.

Built in 1923 with an upstairs ballroom as a reminder of the time when big bands served the Oakland party crowd, the former J. J. Newberry Company is located at 1933 Broadway. Another outstanding Art Deco building, the Floral Depot building, flashing a silver and cobalt blue exterior, is located around the corner at Telegraph Avenue and Nineteenth Street. Built in 1931, the building stands because the Oakland Heritage Alliance fought to keep it from being torn down for a mall.

Across the street is perhaps the most fabulous of downtown buildings, the Fox Theatre, with its design weaving together Hindu and Islamic motifs. Once a movie palace and concert hall where stars such as Bing Crosby and Ginger Rogers performed, it accommodated traveling Broadway shows with huge casts on its stage, larger than that of the Paramount, according to Annalee. After it closed in the 1970s, it was purchased by a private citizen for $340,000. The city's office of redevelopment later bought it for $1 million, typically its good intentions arriving a day late and with a price to pay. The current administration is attempting to woo a developer.

FROM THE FOX, we stroll to the Kaiser building. From 1868 to 1957 it was the site of the College of Holy Names and junipers, pansies, petunias, and lilies of the Nile planted by the sisters still bloom in its rooftop garden. The curves of the building were meant to complement those of Lake Merritt, which it overlooks.

Like so many Oaklanders, Henry Kaiser was from New York but came west in the 1920s to make his money paving roads and building ships, industries that attracted thousands of workers. Working with a physician named Sidney Greenfield to create a prepaid group insurance program for the sudden surge of workers at his shipyards during World War II, Kaiser established the nation's original HMO for the benefit of his workers. When the war ended and the shipyards slowed down, the program, largely supported by unions, was opened to the public. Kaiser himself made the decision to build the company's headquarters in Oakland instead of San Francisco.

Our tour group tromps over to the edge of the rooftop garden, where there is a view of Lake Merritt. Annalee calls

Lake Merritt the heart and soul of Oakland, but the usual name given it by Oakland's residents is "the jewel." Once part of poor Don Luis Peralta's property under the Spanish land grant, the lake was formed in 1869 when a dam was built north of the Twelfth Street bridge. In 1870 Governor Henry Haight signed a bill making the lake the first wildlife refuge in North America and in 1874 it was called Merritt, in honor of Dr. Samuel Merritt, one of the city's early mayors. In 1876 the Camron-Stanford house was built as a speculative house on the lakeshore north of Twelfth Street.

Other landmarks surrounding or near the lake include the Art Deco–style Scottish Rite Temple, built in 1926 and remodeled in 1938–1939, and the Beaux Arts–style Veterans Memorial Building, completed in 1928. In 1913 a necklace of lights was strung around the lake in observance of California Admission Day. In 1941, after the bombing of Pearl Harbor, the lights were turned off because of concerns that the necklace could double as a bull's-eye for Japanese bombers. In 1987, after citizens raised $1 million, the lights were turned on again, a sign of the devotion that common Oaklanders have for their lake, as well as of their desire to keep it adorned in glory.

Lake Merritt is the largest urban saltwater lake in the United States, but before it was dammed it was part of the larger San Francisco Bay. And that bay, of course, preceded Mayor Merritt and even the Peralta family. After the tour, I talk to publisher Malcolm Margolin, author of the classic *The Ohlone Way,* to get a view of what the San Francisco Bay looked like when a European first set eyes upon it.

The Portola expedition was on land looking for Monterey Bay and they had already passed it. They came instead to Pacifica. It was a foot expedition and they could see the Farallon Islands from there and that was a known navigational point. So they stopped to take sights and then sent a Sergeant Ortega up to the hills to hunt for deer. He went up to the top of the hills to where Crystal Springs Reservoir is now. It was the first view that any outsider had of San Francisco Bay.

He talked about it as this "immense arm of the sea." Looking down to the Santa Clara Valley, you saw this big, grassy savanna, with these big broad open areas of dark oak trees, Guadalupe Creek, Coyote Creek, big grasslands. If you looked toward Oakland and south of Oakland you could see the Alviso marshes, the biggest marshland on the Pacific Coast. It was huge court grass, it was the pickled weeds, it was swampy areas. One of the things that developers do when they come in is they like solid land you can build on. They like deep water that you could run ships into. Back then the difference between land and sea wasn't all that clear. Here were areas that were all marshes. I suspect that the whole area between Alameda Island and Oakland was called the estuary—that the whole area was full of marshes that got drained.

Lake Merritt was open to the water, and the marshes extended into Lake Merritt. The whole area that is now Oakland Airport was just big, vast marshes. You'd have channels running through the marshes. Lake Merritt was connected to the bay. It was salt water. There is a tunnel that runs from the lake underneath Laney College, and you still have water coming in and going out. But it's now been channelized, so it is no longer this kind of swampy water seeping in. It is all thick with vegetation. It was thick with wildlife. It was a major place on the Pacific flyway. When the birds come south for the winter they don't just spread out, they come in air channels. There are geese and ducks coming in from Alaska, Canada, and Siberia. They come in over Alaska and down. They have routes that they take, and they stop in certain places for the winter. One of those routes is right here in the Bay Area, right up through the Carquinez Strait and San Pablo Bay and down into Oakland and off toward San Jose.

The Europeans talk about how the air was darkened with the flight of geese and ducks. They talk about how if you came into the swamps and shot off a rifle, the sounds of the birds rising up was like a hurricane. It was just a flapping and it was thick with bird life. Then you would have a marshy area and get into the flatlands, places with thick, tall grass and animals like pronghorn antelope and tule elk, and down to the marshes and back again. You would also have different kinds of oak forests around Alameda. Oakland had an open forest, called an ensenal by the Spanish, that was big, broad grassland almost like a park. There is an old painting of Oakland that shows oak groves near Madison and Thirteenth. It shows these big, beautiful oak trees. Oak trees have always been here. Live oaks that kept their leaves all year round. Other wildlife at the time included grizzly bears, condors, bald eagles, deer, wolves, and mountain lions. Plentiful game was seasonably available. You also had salmon coming up. A lot of these creeks, like the San Leandro and Strawberry Creeks, had coho *salmon. There were salmon in Oakland. The salmon are out in the ocean, but then they'd come to spawn, to lay their eggs, they come up to the rivers of their birth. Alameda Creek, San Leandro Creek, Strawberry Creek, and Temescal Creek. Those were the big creeks. Because of development, and over-fishing, they no longer run freely; the water runs in tubes underneath the ground. In the eyes of the people who did it, this was a great boon to humanity, this was a civic improve-ment, this was getting rid of malarial swamps, this was getting rid of places that were useless to human habitation, where there was nothing but fierce and disgusting animals. Nobody wanted grizzly bears, wolves, coyotes, and foxes.*

While Margolin gives a poetic and rapturous account of the early landscape, naturalist Stephanie Benevides displays a different kind of devotion to it. Benevides, the historian of Lake Merritt and the lake's most rigorous advocate in her work for the Lake Merritt Wildlife Refuge, informs me that Lake Merritt was the first wildlife refuge in North America, established 132 years ago. "We're the first in the nation; we're older than Yosemite and Yellowstone, and we pre-ceded the federal refuges, which will celebrate their one hundredth anniversaries in the year 2003." According to Benevides, early writers described the lake as a slew and a cesspool, and the Oakland Auditorium sits on the landfill that was dredged out of Lake Merritt to dam it and make it a lake. The lake sits on a tide plain of salt water, a floodplain, and it was actually an estuary cradle where fish came to spawn. She continues:

Along the northern Pacific coast the watersheds that supported migrating geese have been taken over by city populations and are now golf courses and parks. It's hard to tell geese that after millions of years, that's not your land anymore. The geese have been slow to get the message. When they do land on a golf course or a park, or in somebody's backyard, people send their dogs after them; they put out all these devices to force them to leave, which pushes them farther down until they come to Lake Merritt. Well, let me tell you, the geese population at Lake Merritt is not a result of the offspring; we have thirty-seven this year. It's actually the result of the geese trying to find a safe place before they lose all their flight feathers for six weeks and become land-bound. All of those dogs and those things that try to chase them off can't succeed because the geese are unable to fly until September. When they become land-bound, which corresponds with their time of nesting, they can't go anywhere.

After the land was taken away from the Peraltas, who were given these huge land grants, there were three men who came in: Carpentier, Moon, and Adams. Two of them were lawyers, and they saw potential here. They went to poor old Peralta and said, "Let me lease four hundred and fifty acres from you. We'll help you take care of it." Peralta said, "Okay, fine," and then one day Peralta was out there with his son and they saw all of these people and said, "Hey, where did all you people come from? This is our land." They said, "We bought it from Carpentier, Moon, and Adams." So little by little, even though the courts agreed that the land belonged to the Peraltas, they lost it to all these people coming in, and pretty soon Oakland became a city in 1850. From then on it's been nonstop. One of the people who came around 1851 was Samuel Merritt. Samuel Merritt saw Lake Merritt (at the time called Peralta Lake) as the most beautiful spot in the whole world, as did other people. Even though he was in San Francisco, he came over and spent more and more time on this side, the city that held up the bridge at the other end of San Francisco, so to speak, and built his home. He got tired of walking around the lake and seeing one dead cow here, one dead bird there, and decided he wanted to protect it. Men back then were visionaries, and they came along and would say: "How do I protect this land?" So he went to Senator Tompson and Governor Haight and they wrote legislation to create a refuge. The legislation was only five paragraphs long. The first part deals with fish, the second part deals with everything else they could think of, every wildlife, bird, and species, and to this day this law still holds true.

We are the future that they protected one hundred and thirty-two years ago. This lake is the future. They said, Protect it for the future. One hundred and thirty-two years later, we are sitting here talking about it. It's part of the life of all the citizens. It's a common denominator in their lives. It doesn't matter what language, what religion—if you have a bag of bread, you can save Lake Merritt, you can save the birds; it's a common denominator. With the help of our citizens it's a showplace for tourists who come to this city.

We have pelicans, brown pelicans, here, but a lot of species disappeared. They disappeared because of disappearing wetlands. Some of the habitats are being restored for bird festivals.

Bird festivals have increased from ten in 1985 to about sixty today, and for one city in Michigan alone, they bring in forty million dollars to boost the economy, in that case just from a sandhill crane festival. So we're seeing some of these birds coming back. But a lot of habitats are not coming back to support them.

I enjoy the lake all day long. It's seasonal. I've been there all these years. Early morning, when I get there, it's really peaceful, the birds are out eating, doing their thing, waking up, standing in the sun. The public then coming around to enjoy the lake are mothers with their strollers, the older people who need time just to sit and walk and exercise. By the afternoon we get a change. You see runners and walkers working off their stress near the buildings and offices there. When you get to around five or six o'clock it changes again with people coming off work to go home; it's a slower pace. When all this is going on, leaves are blooming, the flowers are growing, the bees are happy, the birds are eating. It's such a beautiful campus to see this cycle of life with all these species. People don't like to think of themselves in that sense, but they are a species, they are one of the animals in the city. You say that, and we laugh about that, but when we get to nesting time in the spring, I have to go out and tell people, "Don't throw pine cones, don't throw rocks at the birds. That is normal mating behavior. That is what birds do. It's a shocker."

Well, what they see are ten males chasing one poor female, and they think that's too many. But if the female wanted to get away, she could fly.

California's Indians

T HIS CHAPTER IS a virtual memorial to all the California Indians who died in the many years of genocide.

TIME LINE*

1729–1834—Many populations are captured and forced into slave labor. In the Mission System, soldiers abuse women and spread venereal disease, which repeatedly decimates indigenous populations, as do other diseases, such as measles and smallpox. Friars punish Indians with flogging for any infraction, including running away. Indians build the Mission System at tremendous personal cost.

* One of the sources for this time line was a webpage created as an educational resource on the California genocide of native peoples. Copyright held by Dr. Diane Tuminia, Department of Sociology, California State University at Sacramento.

1769—Father Junípero Serra arrives at San Diego with military support. The Spanish barter with the indigenous peoples. Soldiers build El Presidio, the fort. Some native people convert to Catholicism as part of the trade process; others are forced to work at the mission.

1775—Presidio soldiers pursue two runaways, Zegota and Francisco, who escape and organize a Kumeyaay rebellion, burning Mission San Diego.

1777—Mission Santa Clara measles epidemic.

1782—Mission Santa Barbara is built. The Spanish disrupt the native Chumash economy and spread disease.

1793—The Ohlone people are pressed into service in San Francisco.

1795—Two hundred Indians flee Mission Dolores in San Francisco.

1804—In San Diego, a friar who flogs a cook is poisoned. At Santa Cruz, Indians kill another friar.

1820—Twenty thousand Native Americans are now in the Mission System. Called neophytes, they are mistreated, beaten, sexually assaulted, or killed for infractions, particularly running away.

1824—The Chumash revolt at Santa Barbara, Santa Ines, and La Purisima Concepcion missions.

1834—The governor of California frees Indians from the missions, but without land they are forced into servitude with wealthy landowners. Many migrate to Los Angeles.

1837—Native people are the victims of genocidal raids.

José Maria Amador, Mexican-born Indian fighter, kills two hundred.

1839–1849—Gold prospector Johann Sutter keeps six hundred to eight hundred Indians in virtual slavery.

1847—The Indian district of Los Angeles is razed. Native Americans are required to live with their "masters."

1848—Indians are exploited for gold panning operations.

1849—Weber Creek Massacre.

1849—The Pomo of Clear Lake rise up against their "masters." The army puts down the rebellion.

1850—Bloody Island Massacre.

1850—At the Feather River Massacre, the Miwok are attacked by militia. Antonio Garra, chief of the Cupenos, leads an uprising in Warner Springs against Juan José Warner.

1850–1860—Indians are removed to "farms," or prereservations.

1850–1868—Indians are openly and actively traded as slaves. Children and women are constantly abducted.

1850–1872—The Yahi are hunted and killed. Ishi, the last of the Yahi tribe, survives.

1852—The California legislature authorizes $1.1 million to reimburse people who kill Indians.

1852—Bridge Gulch Massacre.

1855–1856—Miners attack and burn rancherios.

1856—The Hupa Indians are moved to "reservations."

1856–1857—Indians are pushed off their land to mountains.

1859—Women and children are forced to go to the
Mendocino Reservation. Big storms cause starvation
because the Indians fear the flooded waters and are
unable to hunt.

1860—The Indian Island Massacre happens as a result of
the escape of the Wintoons. Forty Indians escaped
from Klamath Reservation now rely on the white
man for the necessities of life.

1860–1890—The reservation system is officially established.

1861—More rancherios are destroyed.

1862—Concow Maidu Trail of Tears begins when the
Concow Maidu leave the Round Valley Reservation
in an ill-fated attempt to return to their old home
in the Sacramento Valley.

1863—The *Humboldt Times* editorializes for extermination.

1863—More rancherios are burned and there are battles at
Willow Creek and Arcata.

1864—There are battles at Redwood Creek and Mad
River, and a fight on the South Salmon River. The
white man keeps the Indians on the move to prevent them from resting and from building up
ammunition. More rancherios are destroyed in
April and July.

1865—Millions of California Indians die due to severe
weather, being taken off their land, starvation, violence, and the destruction of their homes.

1872—Captain Jack of the Modocs is attacked.

1880s—Native American children are forced to go to
"Indian" schools.

1887—The Dawes Act is enacted.

1900—Anthropologist Alfred Kroeber starts his research at the University of California, Berkeley.

1911—Ishi, a Yahi man, is found in Oroville. Ishi would live for the remainder of his life at Berkeley, under the care of Kroeber and others, teaching them about the Yahi.

1950–1960s—The Termination Policy of the federal government is put into effect, in which the government unilaterally dissolved its official relationship with Indian tribes in an effort to force assimilation.

1969—Indians of all nations take over Alcatraz Island.

1972—A petition by American Indian students at Stanford University results in that school's dropping its Indian mascot and logos.

1987—In *California vs. Cabazon Band of Mission Indians,* the Supreme Court rules that the states cannot enforce any gaming laws or regulations on Indian reservations. In response to *California vs. Cabazon,* Congress passes the Indian Gaming Regulatory Act (IGRA) of 1988, which gives states limited power over tribal gaming.

1999—Northern Californian tribes demand the return of Ishi's remains.

2000—Ishi's brain is returned to the Indian people; the Miwok fight to reclaim their tribal status.

2002—California dedicates a bronze plaque on the steps of the Capitol to California Indians.

DECEMBER 7

Tennessee and I drive to Oakland Technical High School for the Third Annual Holiday Powwow. Given the history of the California Indians and their treatment by a succession of invaders, it's amazing that there are enough Indians remaining to hold a powwow. This is the first event that I choose to cover for this book, and it's proper that it should be the first. The Indians were here first. One has to agree with Malcolm Margolin that they were the best ecologists and that things have gone downhill since the land was taken from them by force. Both the Spanish and the Mexicans used them as slave labor, and the atrocities committed by the Americans are such that you can understand why they now use dismissive terms like political correctness to discourage any discussion of this history.

At the powwow we are treated to eagle dances performed by members of different tribes, dances preserved as part of an effort to "perpetuate" their culture. As far as I can tell, the eagle dance involves much jerking of the head and twirling about. The continuity of tradition is also manifested in the manner in which dancers representing different generations form a line. At the head, elders dance in place, followed by their chronological successors; the younger the dancers the wilder the dance. This dance, mimicking the movements of wildlife, shows how much the Indians not only observed the animals around them but actually saw them as fellow beings. Mary Tallmountain, the late poet, referred to a blue whale as

ISHMAEL REED

her "dark sister." I asked Malcolm Margolin about how the
Indians got along with nature. "To the Indian mind there
wasn't a clear distinction between people and animals as we
understand it. Indians lived in a world made by coyotes and
eagles, a world instituted by animal divinities." How many
Indians inhabited the Oakland area when the Europeans
arrived?

> They were a handful. This was one of the most densely popu-
> lated places in North America. On the other hand, you are
> talking about a couple of people per square mile, hunting and
> gathering people who lived in small communities. Maybe if you
> lived in Oakland you would be speaking a language called
> Choshenyo that was spoken by five tribal groups. The tribal
> group around here was called Huichiun. Their language was
> spoken from the Carquinez Strait down to about Fremont. So
> this was the Choshenyo language, probably spoken by no more
> than a thousand people who lived here. If you went to Moraga
> and Lafayette, or to San Francisco or San Jose, there were dif-
> ferent dialects and languages. They were distinct languages.
> These small numbers of people were living in this world where
> there is a density of wildlife, birds, and fish, and eagles and
> grizzly bears and deer and antelope. I don't know if it was
> paradise or not. But what I do know is that you had a strong
> animal presence that we don't have. Other than Rover and
> Tabby we never see any animals. Until this past century you
> would spend time with animals, whether it was the horse
> bringing you somewhere behind the pasture, the cow you were
> milking, the pig you were slaughtering, or the chickens you

were collecting eggs from. You were connected to animals. This is the first generation where you have a majority of people in a country not connected to animals. Humans become important to us because they are what we see. Back then you woke up in the morning to the thick sounds of animals. During the night you would hear crickets. The air becomes thick and powerful and pulsates with the sounds of animal life out there. You would hear the cry of geese and ducks that were coming in, and animals surrounded you. The Indians would skin the bear and they couldn't tell whether it was a man or a bear. The bear had human form. Shamans were supposed to be able to put on bearskins and turn themselves into bears. Part of their power was to travel tremendous distances to poison their enemies. Once I asked this old Indian if they still did this and he said, "No, we don't have to do it anymore."

At the powwow, Tennessee and I visit some of the booths selling everything from healing stones to T-shirts. For lunch, they are selling bowls of chili beans, tamale plates, and Indian tacos. I buy a buffalo burger.

Panthers and Brownies

OCTOBER 4

I TAKE A lunch date with Brenda Payton, *Oakland Tribune* columnist and one of the best American satirists, to check out the Washington Inn, a landmark that was missed on the Old Oakland tour. I learned during the city's gay pride celebration that this is the only gay-owned hotel in town. The Inn, located at 495 Tenth Street in Old Oakland, was built in 1913 by A. W. Smith, a local architect. In her book *The Spirit of Oakland,* Abby Wasserman discusses the outstanding features of this Italianate-style hotel. Its features include double-hung windows, a galvanized iron cornice featuring medallions above each bay, and large-scale brackets. The food is good; I have calamari.

Brenda and I talk politics. She has a sharp intellect and has been a thorn in the side of the two previous black mayors, Elihu Harris and Lionel Wilson. Hearty black western pioneers, her family was spoken of in reverential tones when I talked to some black citizens during a trip to El Paso, Texas. She doesn't spare this mayor. She refers to him as a prince, an appellation with which many of his critics would agree. One writer has described Jerry Brown as "lofty" and "aloof."

Unlike previous mayors Harris and Wilson, who had to face the public each week during council meetings, this mayor has been accused of being removed from the process. On a trip from New York, I sat across the aisle from an Oakland councilman. He said that with Elihu Harris, the relationship between the council and the mayor was different. He would approach Harris and they'd form a consensus about the administration's goals. But this mayor is different. He and his Brownies answer to no one and the enigmatic Jacques Barzaghi represents himself as the man who speaks for the mayor. This style of government would cause difficulties for the mayor in the November election, when several of his projects would be defeated by the voters.

In an imaginary meeting between the Prince and an aide, Payton describes the voters turning down his proposals as "a flogging." Another commentator says that Brown gets most of his support from the affluent, white Oakland hills, where people didn't turn out to vote due to their dissatisfaction with Governor Gray Davis. A measure that would have given the mayor additional power loses. The measure to add one hundred more police to the streets, the one that Bobby Seale and some grassroots activists have opposed, also fails. Their complaint was that the $70 million required to implement such a measure could better be used to fund social programs for teenagers.

On Wednesday, the day after the election, what are described by the *Oakland Tribune* as "anti-police protestors" storm the mayor's office to protest Brown's plans to put the measure up for another vote in the March 2003 election. Payton has some fun with the mayor's announcement that he will reach out and form a consensus, a strategy proposed by one of his critics, Councilwoman Nancy Nadel. He is also chastised by an *Oakland Tribune* editorial: "We think that the message was a wake-up call to Brown, whose popularity may have been dinged by his failing to be more accessible to citizens and by his aloofness toward community issues that don't capture his attention."

On November 5, on KPFA radio, Wilson Riles Jr., Jerry Brown's rival in the election, says that Brown's aim is to drive African-Americans from Oakland. *Street Spirit,* published by the American Friends Service Committee, is jubilant about the success of measure EE, called the "Just Cause Measure" and intended to preserve the diversity of Oakland from the corrupting influence of gentrification and the eviction-for-profit system. "Low-income families living in rental housing no longer have to live in constant fear of receiving no-cause evictions," and their children have gained a new measure of security that they won't be driven out of their homes and schools. Protected from the tyranny of Oakland's notorious landlords, the retired elderly citizens who helped build this town may now bask in their golden years free from the fear of the dreaded no-cause eviction notice.

OCTOBER 6

Today I drive over to De Fremery Park for the Black Panther picnic. At first I think that I've made a mistake, maybe getting the date of the picnic confused, because I don't see a crowd. Back in the 1960s the Panthers used to pack this park with thousands of people. Media from around the world covered their every utterance. Today there's one lone interviewer from KALX, the University of California's student-operated radio station. I spot a humble gathering beneath a tree and park my car.

Some young women are serving barbecued ribs and chicken and potato salad, picnic staples. I grab a plate. There are a lot of gray heads, beaded hats, and T-shirts. One woman wears a T-shirt emblazoned with photos of Notorious Biggie Smalls and Tupac Shakur, two martyrs of a different generation—one, Tupac, the child of a Panther and a son of Oakland (via New York, again). Oversized framed photos, placed next to the tree, recall the glory days of the Panthers. One is the famous photo of Panther founders Bobby Seale and the late Huey Newton, dressed in black leather and the trademark berets, brandishing rifles. Another photo shows the late Bobby Hutton and Bobby Seale armed and wearing their Panther uniforms (berets and leather), entering the California legislature. In another iconic shot we see Huey Newton, proud and soulful in a butterfly chair. David Hilliard, a former Panther chief of staff, points out some of the old-timers: Emory Douglas, Sherman Forte, Steve McCutheon, Brendy Presley, Shirley Sanders, Terry Cotton—all veterans of the Panther wars. This is the group that drove J. Edgar Hoover to use illegal tactics, including murder, to destroy the party, and Richard Nixon to create the very secretive measures that would eventually drive him from office.

There are a number of children, many of them, like the early Californios (the term for California-born New Spaniards), of mixed heritage. They're bright. It's apparent that they live in homes where books are present. One of the teenagers is named Lafiea. She's reading the autobiography of Assatta Shakur and points to a passage in the book about how God has abandoned African-Americans. Shakur lives in Cuba now, a fugitive after escaping from a New Jersey prison after her conviction for the murder of a police officer. Lafiea asks me to explain the passage to her. I ramble and stumble around an explanation for about ten minutes before giving up.

Old friends who haven't seen each other in years embrace. There are Asian-Americans in attendance as well. One sits at our table. She's not a former Panther, but has come because of her cause: police brutality. At about 3:30 P.M. the stout figure of Bobby Seale ambles toward the crowd. He's returned to Oakland and is considering a run for a city council seat. It was his strong showing in a contest for mayor in 1973 that opened the door for black power in Oakland politics.

The following week Seale is in the newspapers. He's opposed to Jerry Brown's plan to put one hundred additional police on the streets of Oakland. Later this month some teenagers will appear on KPFA radio, also opposing the plan. They'll say that they had arranged a meeting with the mayor for which the mayor didn't show, his explanation being that his time was precious. It will turn out that he was attending a Raiders game.

One of the teenagers on KPFA, a Southeast Asian girl, will say that Southeast Asian kids are also harassed by the Oakland police, which will probably come as a surprise for those media people in the East who view all Asian-American groups as "model minorities." When I interview Frank Chin, he'll say that crime has always been a problem in Chinatown and some of the upright citizens who condemn crimes committed by newcomers made their fortunes in prostitution. While the TV networks and the Hollywood industry entertain their audiences with shows about black pimps, the fact that fifty-five thousand women are imported into the country, many from Asia, for prostitution is ignored.

OCTOBER 27

Carla, Tennessee, and I drive over to the Fruitvale district for the Seventh Annual Dia de Los Muertos (Day of the Dead) Festival. The Day of the Dead rites begin in October and end the first week in November. The streets are crowded with Mexican-American families headed toward International Boulevard for the festivities. Along the way, we find altars to deceased relatives placed before residences. Once there, we find the same booths, both profit and non-profit, that we've found at all the other street fairs and festivals. Though there continues to be an English-only drive in the West, corporations apparently haven't heard about it. Washington Mutual Bank, for example, advertises in Spanish, and though some white male western writers like to swash-buckle about in attire created by Mexicans, this Mexican-American crowd's favorite fashions are T-shirts and jeans, globalization's uniform. We're watching the whole thing in front of a travel agency that advertises trips to Guadalajara for $368. Five stages present such acts as Banda Bahia, the Caterpillar Puppets, Red Eye Gypsy, and Loco Bloco. We catch a Tex-Mex singer named Reyna Santilla, but the Aztec dancers are the highlight of the performance. Dressed in tradi-tional costumes, they perform a kinetic bird dance, similar to the eagle dance at the powwow, all but flying away themselves.

NOVEMBER 8

The winter is upon us. Power lines are down and twenty-one thousand locals are without power. There are fifty-mile-per-hour gusts. Nevertheless, about two hundred people brave the weather to attend a ceremony in which the Oakland Heritage Alliance will honor the African-American Museum and Library in Oakland. Jerry Brown, smitten by the election, is scheduled to speak. When I arrive, the rooms of the library are crowded with people awaiting the arrival of the mayor. As I stand in the children's library room, Michael Willis enters. We are introduced. He is the architect who led the restoration of this Beaux Arts building that had been heavily damaged by the Loma Prieta earthquake of 1989. He says that putting the building back together was like "fixing a

Swiss watch. The walls were on the floor." During the official program, held on the second floor, a speaker says that the ceiling was on the floor. Either way, the place was a mess.

Andrew Carnegie built five libraries in Oakland at the cost of $50,000 each. This one was his pride. At the time of the earthquake, the building was being used as surplus office space. Michael Willis says that the room in which we are standing is one of the few structures from the original building, built in 1903 and opened in 1909. It was designed by Bliss and Faville. The city needed a sponsor so that the building might be restored, and the Oakland Public Library stepped forward.

The mayor finally arrives with an entourage of Brownies and the ceremony begins. I was present in the chambers of the state legislature one day in 1979 when a handsome Jerry Brown and a stunning, tanned Jane Fonda strode in. Those were the California glamour days. There was a $2 billion surplus. The actor Peter Coyote was chairing a meeting of the California Arts Council and thanked me for coming to California. Now the former governor has developed a paunch; Tennessee says that with the fuzz on his neck, the bald spot surrounded by thinning hair, and the beak nose, he looks like a bald eagle.

Councilperson Nancy Nadel speaks first. She was one of those responsible for the building's rejuvenation. She says that she'd driven by the abandoned building often. She and others wanted to do something for this Oakland landmark, but were stymied by bureacrats. Brown next steps to the microphone and makes some offhand remarks. About the building, he says that "the old is part of the new" and that it was "very nice." His remark that "all of us preservationists must work together" draws some laughs from the propreservation crowd. Brown's development hunger has often clashed with their plans. His remark that "in five years they will be placing a plaque before my commune" draws a heckler. "I don't think so," someone else says. With his head down, Brown leaves the ceremony along with his entourage. This has probably been his worst week as Oakland's mayor.

The guests are asked to go upstairs for the formal presentation of heritage awards. On the second floor we're confronted with neoclassical grandeur, an attempt by those who had conquered the Californios and the Native Americans to transplant European civilization to what they called "the frontier." The room features Corinthian columns and names of classical scholars engraved in stone. There are murals by early-twentieth-century painters Arthur F. Matthew and Marion Holdon. Architect Michael Willis had told us, when we were standing in the children's room earlier, that the style of pediments and round-patterned wood paneling atop the bookcases is after Michelangelo. So dedicated to restoring this building were some of the workers, they postponed their retirements. With this building, western civ is putting on the dog, and although one might find the jump-up structures built for the 10Kers ugly in their functionality, at least some of their designs have more indigenous references. Some buildings on Powell Street in Emeryville, located near the Amtrak station, for example, resemble Native American cliff dwellings.

When, during the presentation of awards by the heritage alliance, Michael Willis points critically to the names of dead white males, which occupy a place of prominence on the walls, there is murmuring from some of the members of the audience. One woman behind me says, "That's the way it should be." Another chimes in "Why not; it's the history of mankind." Willis says that the names of Duke Ellington, Romare Bearden, and Quincy Troupe should replace these. More murmuring in the audience, 80 percent of which is white. But never mind that; this event has the best buffet so far, catered by Ratto's International Market, Everett and Jones Barbecue, Trader Joe's, and Your Black Muslim Bakery. Eats galore. The music is provided by the Oaktown Jazz Workshops. Some of the musicians, including a black girl on drums, haven't reached their teens. Clifford Brown Jr., the master of ceremonies, calls on Jerry Brown to speak, but is informed that Brown has taken off for the Rolling Stones concert. Brown and the Brownies and the 10Kers are the sort of people who voted the Stones' "(I Can't Get No) Satisfaction" the top rock-and-roll song of the twentieth century and would approve of Bobby Dylan's receiving the W. C. Handy Blues Award. Mary McDonald, president of the twenty-one-year-old Oakland Heritage Alliance, presents a number of individuals and organizations, including Rick Ross, the museum's curator, with awards.

Ross and I were guests on a broadcast of "West Coast Live" on local PBS affiliate KQED. After the broadcast, I made arrangements to interview him for this book. So there I was, early one morning, standing outside of the library at the agreed-upon time of 9:00 A.M. No Ross. I waited for some library personnel and left a message for him. He never called.

This type of Oakland experience so frustrates some artists that they depart for New York. The people in Oakland who have the power to promote culture and the arts don't seem that comfortable with artists, which may explain why the cultural capital of the United States is New York and why the West Coast has the reputation of a place that doesn't initiate anything but trite, formulaic, multinational packaged movies held together with predictable gadgetry and stunts like car chases. After a spiteful, ignorant review of our opera *Gethsemane Park* by a San Francisco critic, New York composer Carman Moore said that he could see why talent is strangled on the West Coast and not much of it gets beyond the Rockies. If it were not for Berkeley's Black Repertory Theater, some of us would have nowhere out here to produce our plays.

The speeches and acceptances continue until a speaker comes to the podium, someone who isn't even listed on the program: ninety-two-year-old Gladys Jordan, who steals the show. She's a member of the Northern California Center for African-American History and Life, the antecedent of the African-American Library and Museum. Founded sixty years ago by Oaklanders who believed that the history of African-Americans in the West was not being told, the center counted among its members Morris Turner, the creator of the popular cartoon "Wee Pals." Ms. Jordan was introduced by Melvin Terry, the president of the museum's board of trustees.

Clifford Brown Jr. next introduces ex–California poet laureate Quincy Troupe. He has become ex- within the last month, after being exposed for puffing his résumé. (He had said that he had a B.A. from Grambling State University, which was not true.) People are wondering how he will respond—to the exposure, and to the flurry of newspaper stories, many of them critical. A reporter for the *San Diego Union* even got hold of his transcript and found that Troupe had attended Grambling for only a semester, which also happens to be the amount of time that Jack London attended college. But Troupe has contributed much to the artistic life of La Jolla, his California home, and San Diego, both the University of California campus and the city; even the *San Diego Union* said so, claiming it would be a tragedy for San Diego if Troupe were to return to the East.

Perhaps that's why Quincy and his wife, Margaret, bound into the museum as though nothing had happened. Both Tucker Carlson, who, according to David Brock's recent book, *Blinded by the Right,* has no convictions and says things for money (yet he calls Johnny Cochran repulsive), and the man who is supposed to be his left-wing debating opponent on *Crossfire,* Paul Begala, had some laughs about Troupe and the condition of Amiri Baraka, poet laureate of New Jersey, also under fire this month for suggesting in a poem that the Israeli and the United States governments knew about the terrorist attack on the World Trade Center before it happened. I doubt whether four thousand people of any ethnic group can keep a secret, but I was really annoyed by the tone and sarcasm of the *Crossfire*

duo as they belittled the accomplishments of Troupe and
Baraka. I had met Amiri in the mid-1960s and Troupe in
1969. With Steve Cannon, I published Troupe's second and
third books of poetry. I published Amiri's controversial
Sidney Poet Heroical and have his book of concrete poetry in
production. Annoyed? I was burning up. The Don Imus
formula has been picked up by cable networks CNN and
MSNBC. In order to attract an audience that enjoys insult-
ing black people, Imus has Bernard McGirk tell "nigger
jokes." The cable networks have buttoned-down versions of
McGirk and his lowlife vulgarian colleagues. Their assign-
ment seems to be that of playing "gotcha" on black people
as a technique for boosting ratings. So desperate was CNN's
Walter Issacson to draw some of Fox News's "conservative"
audience that after Jack White called David Horowitz, a
professional and well-paid black basher, a "racist," Issacson
visited Horowitz's Los Angeles organization, which is supported by funds from people like Richard Mellon Scaife,
and kissed his ring. At Salon.com it's Attack Queer Andrew
Sullivan. At CNN it's Tucker Carlson, whose comments
about Jesse Jackson, Al Sharpton, and Michael Jackson are
aimed at an audience that gets cheap thrills by hearing black
bashers depict black men as buffoons.

But later I thought, how many times do young black
people see a black male writer mentioned on the networks?
Black men only show up in the sports, entertainment, and
crime sections of the media. Poet Al Young calls to tell me
that *The New Yorker* has picked up the story about Troupe,
which could also be seen as a plus, because how often do you

see a black poet mentioned in *The New Yorker,* published by Don Imus's buddy David Remnick? During the time when Carlson and his opponent on the left, Begala, ridiculed Troupe and Baraka, CNN ran a story about a black man selling PCP and one about a black basketball player punching a white basketball player. The footage showing the punch was repeated dozens of times. Also, hours were devoted to discussing Michael Jackson's plastic surgery. So any mention of two serious black male writers under any circumstances, I felt, was an improvement over the way black men are usually represented.

Having entered the museum beaming and sparkling in their designer outfits, African-American culture's first couple seem unfazed by the publicity, and when I tell Troupe of the mention on *Crossfire,* he says he hasn't heard about it. Ever fashion-conscious, Troupe wears a black Senegalese suit designed by Mustafa Kilamanjaro Fashions in Harlem, and Margaret a black Donna Karan suit with a beige silk scarf designed by Garance.

None of the speakers mention the other library, at one time the Oakland Free Library and located downtown, where City Hall now stands. It was a resource and inspiration for Jack London, who wrote, "I would go up to the Free Library, exchange my books, buy a quarter's worth of all sorts of candy that chewed and lasted, sneak aboard the *Razzle Dazzle,* lock myself in the cabin, go to bed, and lie there long hours of bliss, reading and chewing candy." Jack London's guide at the library was Ina Coolbrith, a poet and major figure in California's literary history. She was reported to be the first white child to enter California through the Beckworth Pass in the saddle of a horse ridden by black California legend Jim Beckworth.

DECEMBER 13

It's raining and the winds are so heavy that they knock the tiles off my neighbor's roof. We're to meet David Hilliard at the Full Moon Restaurant, a Chinese restaurant located in Jack London Square, where he will take us on the Black Panther tour. Hilliard calls about an hour before lunch to say that the tour has been canceled due to the rain, but we decide to meet anyway. We show up to find that the Full Moon Restaurant, an all-you-can-eat place, has moved to Mac-Arthur Boulevard, so we decide on Everett and Jones Barbecue. David orders beef links. Tennessee has barbecued ribs. I have barbecued chicken and clean my plate. David leaves about two-thirds of his links untouched, which must account for his lean appearance. He maintains a thirty-inch waist and still has the same dark handsome looks he had when he started to climb the ladder of the Panthers thirty years ago. Tennessee is still grinning from when he called her a celebrity and said that he and Fredricka, his wife (and the former wife of Huey Newton), had been following her career.

He starts by telling me about a film that's to be shown the following day at the Roxie theater.

I directed a film on the Panthers' Survivor Program. It is a film that addresses economic development programs, the foun-

dation of our organization. We were working with about eight or ten Berkeley High School students, addressing the issues of political prisoners, police brutality, free health clinics, and housing. There are little-known facts about the Black Panthers. There is an eighty-unit apartment on Fifth Avenue under the leadership of Elaine Brown. It's in the film. They were replacement units when City Center was constructed. What is City Center now used to be houses. They were displaced. City Center was funded through the Oakland Economic Development and the Oakland Housing Program (at twelve million dollars). The City Center project was a form of black removal. It was accelerated under Jerry Brown. Jerry Brown's agenda hasn't been affordable housing. The corporate real estate brokers who came to this city made housing very expensive. I endorsed Jerry Brown because he had a message that spoke to the issues that we supported. He started talking about the 10K plan after he won the election. This was not something he said during his campaign. It was his progressive politics that we were supporting. I think that was his game. These politicians have no principles. I talked to him and worked with him before he was elected. He was talking about affordable housing, jobs, community and economic development. His program was the banner he campaigned around when he got elected. His agenda has been totally destructive. It hasn't helped the black community. It seems that Jacques Barzaghi [the mayor's mentor] is reactionary. He is Jerry's close confidant. Maybe there are some big secrets between him and Jerry. Jacques Barzaghi does not represent anything that I consider positive in terms of any policy. What does he do?

Jacques Barzaghi, Jerry Brown's mentor for over thirty years, was the former head of Oakland's cultural arts program. After a sexual harassment scandal for which the city had to pay $50,000, he was given the job of Brown's senior adviser at a salary of $100,000. Hilliard continued talking about his own plans for the city.

Under my program there are agendas on things such as jobs, housing, police oppression. Pretty much the programs that Panthers stood for in the sixties are our unfinished agenda. The breakfast program was relatively successful. When you talk about issues such as police oppression and affordable housing and gentrification, unemployment, health care, civil rights, these are the kind of issues that led to the rise of the Black Panther party. Those issues are pretty much what the FBI hated. We were always on the FBI and the CIA's enemy list. They fought the Panthers more so than any other civil rights organization. That caused the demise of our movement. They went after us and destroyed our movement. Nixon unleashed the COINTELPRO against us with Attorney General Mitchell, J. Edgar Hoover, that whole FBI apparatus. The white left abandoned us. Cleaver came and joined us. He came out of the penitentiary. He was a star because he had a national best-seller.

The media likes to claim that the Black Panthers started as a result of police brutality, but to put it in historical perspective, police brutality was number seven on our agenda. There were six other agenda points before that one. Decent housing, education, health; police brutality was number seven.

We had a problem with the police, but they weren't a serious problem to us like economics were. The Panthers had an international agenda. We weren't racist or nationalist. We embraced everybody. We always worked with the white left, but the white left got taken over. They had no agenda. What is the white left? Jerry Brown? There is no such thing. I think that the white left is the Democratic party and the Green party. I think that there needs to be a political change, but that won't happen overnight. Our philosophy was that revolution was a process. It seems that we have had a setback since Brown vs. the Board of Education. *We are not very advanced since the days when we could barely eat in the restaurants with white folks.*

Hilliard now organizes the Black Panther Legacy tours.

On our tour we do eighteen sites. The first is on Fifty-fifth and Market and we go around to places like Merritt College and to other historical landmarks. The Panthers started in 1966. Huey Newton came by my house after a few police brutality incidents. In Newark [California], a kid was killed by a police officer for stealing. It was in the newspaper. It was the turning point for me to do something. This was around 1963. So my consciousness came around all of this. Huey and I grew up together. I was twenty-three when he came to my house. He came with a white kid and an Asian kid. The Asian guy came with guns. We got national attention when we went up to Sacramento, to the statehouse. Ronald Reagan was out on the lawn talking to some young Republicans and he saw me and ran. This story hasn't been told. The white kids came up to us. The government's job was to reduce us to criminals. COINTELPRO wanted to criminalize us because we had the support of African-American youth. Nixon wanted to get rid of us in 1969. David Horowitz was a friend, a fund-raiser, and more than that. He raised money for our schools. Later he promoted himself as an insider. But he was a white man, and he had no credibility. He became the FBI's voice.

Hilliard goes on to explain that it was the Panthers who put Oakland on the map. "When I first went to New York back in the 1960s to get support, they didn't even know Oakland existed. The event in Sacramento, taking guns to the statehouse, that made Oakland a global name. Before people only knew L.A. and San Francisco. Recently I took a group of white kids from the California College of Arts and Crafts on a bus tour of Oakland. Afterward they complained to the mayor that they had no idea why Oakland didn't have reminders of the Panthers." We suggest to David that we arrange for a private tour of the Panther sites and he agrees. A week later he calls and says that there will be a tour on Saturday. We are to meet at Adeline and Eighteenth Street.

DECEMBER 16

Today Tennessee and I show up for our tour of the Fruitvale district with Councilman Ignacio De La Fuente, the only Latino councilman in the city of Oakland. The Mexican-American population in Oakland is the fastest-growing in

California, surpassing that of San Jose. A 2002 story in the *Oakland Tribune* includes some dramatic statistics: "The Mexican population in Oakland and surrounding areas, which includes U.S. citizens and immigrants, is close to a half a million, making it the second largest community in California and the fifth largest in the United States." We pack into the councilman's black Lincoln and head toward Jingletown, a small village within the Fruitvale district located at East Ninth, Tenth, and Eleventh Streets and inhabited by 98 percent Latino residents. The Portuguese were here first, their presence recalled when we pass a street named Lisbon. African-Americans followed the Portuguese into this district, but now it's clearly a Mexican-American neighborhood. Unemployment is up here because the source of income, heavy and light manufacturing jobs, has relocated to cheaper labor markets or is being replaced by hi-tech industry. De La Fuente points to a glass company that once provided three hundred to four hundred jobs and Vulcan Steel, which at one time was the source of three thousand jobs. Johnson Propeller has left, as has Lucas Manufacturing. Ninety percent of the latter's employees were from the neighborhood and 80 percent of its workers were women. The largest employer in the 1980s was the Del Monte cannery, which is gone, too. De La Fuente says that NAFTA has caused industries to move abroad for cheaper labor. Two million jobs have been exported from the United States within the last two years, a trend that began fifty years ago; moreover, many California agribusinesses are now raising their crops abroad and only processing them here.

He talks about how Latinos have transformed the community. For example, he points to what was once a quarter-pound-burger restaurant that is now run by Latinos. De La Fuente, a utilitarian, parts company with the preservationists. He believes that landmark, or "orchid," buildings should be demolished in order to make way for schools, senior citizens' homes, shopping malls. Locked into a struggle with preservationists over the fate of the Montgomery Ward building, which they wanted to designate a landmark, De La Fuente prevailed and the developer, now building a high school on the site, has promised to include a public soccer field. "So that the commuters will spend some money in the Fruitvale instead of hopping on BART to San Francisco," De La Fuente also counts among those promoting a new multi-use development at the Fruitvale BART station.

De La Fuente points to International Boulevard, the main street of his district, with pride. Not a single boarded-up store here, he boasts. He also points to the Fruitvale Station Mall, which includes a Starbucks, which, he says, was negotiated by Magic Johnson. De La Fuente has one of the most interesting stories we've heard so far.

When I came to this country I came to Washington State. I was a local soccer player back home, and a team offered me a chance to play up there. So I flew to Washington State. I started playing and they gave me fifty dollars a week. They were supposed to get me a job, but they gave me a lousy one cleaning up bathrooms. I didn't like that job so I said, "Either you give me a new job or I leave." I guess they didn't believe me because I had nowhere to go. I had no family. They didn't give me another job after a month, so I went to the airport. With my limited English, I looked at the first flight, and the first flight was to Oakland. All of my family is in Mexico City except for one of my brothers. In Mexico my mom is a high school teacher. She told me to find this family with two boys who were her students. They were in Oakland. I think they worked at a restaurant. They weren't in the phone book, so I started walking around Mexican restaurants looking for them. I found them. They actually gave me a place to stay at 933 Wood Street in West Oakland, which was one of the last streets in West Oakland. I stayed with them for a little while, then I went on my own. I found an apartment and I got a job washing dishes at the Broadway Shopping Center on MacArthur Boulevard. Then I became a cook. My father died when I was ten years old so I had to cook and clean for seven brothers and sisters back in Mexico. In Oakland I was a cook for about a year and a half. The guy who owned the restaurant was a gambler and he lost two restaurants in a year and a half. I started looking around for more jobs and I found one at a foundry. I got hired in 1973. I participated in a huge demonstration for a promotion in 1976. The bosses and machinists were mostly white. The idea was, I wanted to get a promotion based on merit and not on race. I became a leader of the strike and I got elected to the union, the International Welders and Allied Workers Union. This was eight years after I arrived. We won the strike and for the first time we had blacks and Latinos who became apprentices, machinists, and welders, the top-paying positions. I got elected to the union in

1978 and in 1980 I got elected to be the business manager. In 1978, out of eighteen business managers, two business agents, and the executive director, the union leadership was all Italian. There were no blacks or Latinos. We put together a slate. We had eight Latinos and ten blacks to run for the eighteen positions. We won seventeen out of the eighteen positions. This totally changed the faces of people who ran the union. There are only eight members now. We represented all the steel mills and foundries in northern California. I became well known so I got elected to run the union. I started getting into politics by supporting candidates and getting involved with the problems of the city. I went to the Oakland City Council for the very first time in 1985. There were three hundred people behind me, and we stormed into the City Hall chambers. We were losing jobs and no one was doing anything about it. Lionel Wilson was the mayor. We asked him what he was going to do about this and he didn't have an agenda. I decided to come up with one myself so I ran for city council in 1987. Frank Ogawa was at large and I ran against him. I picked Frank Ogawa because I didn't want to run against an African-American. I lost.

I learned from my first term not to trust what people tell you. I learned the hard way. I ran a second time in 1992 against a popular member who is now a city council member in Alameda. He moved there after he left.

Tennessee asks whether the older and younger generations get along. "There is no tension between the older and newer generations in the Latino population. They have different things to offer, but they wouldn't make it without each other," De La Fuente says.

He's critical of some Hispanic organizations.

The Hispanic Chamber of Council don't raise money, they just have parties. I told them I didn't like the way they ran things. I still find African-Americans on the city council. There were more ten years ago than in 2002. We support each other. What I find more troubling is that there were no Latinos elected to BART, AC Transit, the East Bay Regional Park District, and East Bay MUD [the water company]. One was elected to AC Transit during the last term. There haven't been Latinos in many of the government jobs. We are trying to make an election where we don't run against each other. The school board had one Latino in 1992. It's just stupid. We have to find a way for Asians and Latinos to win elections that is not at the expense of African-Americans. I think we lost the Latinos who moved to the suburbs. I think that in order to keep the Latinos here in Oakland we have to improve the conditions. We don't have much racism against Latinos locally, but statewide and nationally, forget about it. We did damage with Propositions 187, 209, and 227. Nancy Nadel and I are writing a resolution against Bush's Patriot Act tomorrow night at City Hall because it's an attack on people of color. This act is used as a tool to continue inter- rogations and investigations.

De La Fuente speaks to us while intermittently taking calls on his cell phone. He seems to know everybody in his district. Like many Latinos, his Indo-African heritage is obvious and he makes no secret of it, unlike some of the earlier Californios who tried to bond with the American invaders on the basis of a common European heritage, but to no avail.

On June 6, 1846, a gang of thugs calling themselves Bear Flaggers entered the home of General Mariano Vallejo in Sonoma. Vallejo, described as "the Americanos best friend," tried to be nice about it. He offered the Bear Flaggers some wine and retired to put on a fancy outfit while they drafted the "articles of capitulation." They took him, his brother, and son-in-law to Fort Sutter and turned them over to John Frémont, a man who nowadays would be considered a gang leader, and his Bear Flag Republic emblem a gang color. They were held incommunicado for months, their visitors were arrested, and their personal belongings were stolen. Vallejo objected to being called "a greaser" by the Bear Flaggers on the grounds that he was of the "purest blood of Europe."

Bluesmen, Gay Pride, and the Heathen Chinee

PLAIN LANGUAGE FROM TRUTHFUL JAMES OR THE HEATHEN CHINEE

by Bret Harte (1870)

Which I wish to remark—
And my language is plain
That for ways that are dark
And for tricks that are vain,
The heathen Chinese is peculiar:
Which the same I would rise to explain.
Ah Sin was his name;
And I shall deny
In regard to the same
What that name might imply;
But his smile it was pensive and childlike,
As I frequent remarked to Bill Nye.

It was August the third,
And quite sort was the skies,
Which it might be inferred
That Ah Sin was likewise;
Yet he played it that day upon William
And me a way I despise.
Which we had a small game,
And Ah Sin took a hand:

It was euchre. The same
He did not understand,
But he smiled, as he sat by the table,
With the smile that was childlike and bland.
Yet the cards they were stocked
In a way that I grieve,
And my feelings were shocked
At the fate of Nye's sleeves,
Which was stuffed full of aces and bowers

And the same intent to deceive.
But the hands that were played
By that heathen Chinee,
And the points that he made,
Were quite frightful to see,—
Till at last he put down a right bower,
Which the same Nye had dealt unto me.
Then I look up at Nye,
And he gazed upon me;
And he rose with a sigh,

And said, Can this be?
We are ruined by Chinese cheap labor
And he went for that heathen Chinee.
In the scene that ensued
I did not take a hand,
But the floor it was stewed,
Like the leaves on the strand,
With the cards flint
Ah Sin had been hiding
In the game he did not understand.
In his sleeves, which were long,
He had twenty-four jacks,——
Which was coming it strong,
Yet I state but the facts.
And we found on his nails, which were taper——
What is frequent in tapers,——that's wax.
Which is why I remark,
And my language is plain,
That for tricks that are vain,
The heathen Chinee is peculiar,——
Which the same I am free to maintain.

Bret Harte called it his worst poem, but the poem reflected
the attitudes of the early, mostly white, male society toward
the Chinese men who began arriving in California at the
time of the Gold Rush. In the model minority game that
some whites in power play with Asian-Americans, Hispanics,
and African-Americans, blacks were considered models of
behavior for Asian-Americans to follow in those days, and

among Asian-Americans, the Japanese were favored over the Chinese before they, like the Chinese before them, were subjected to exclusion laws. Rudyard Kipling's introduction to San Francisco was the sight of a Chinese man running away from a beating. From the time of their arrival in the 1850s and 1860s, the Chinese were subjected to discrimination, exclusion, and even massacres. A few did very well, made money, and returned to China to become landlords; others, less fortunate, remained in the United States and began families. Immigration laws passed after 1882 required that men come alone, and so many of them returned to China to have sons, whom they then brought back to the United States. White men could have any woman they desired of any nationality, but as miscegenephobes (that is, except when it came to their own predilections) they passed laws in 1872 and 1906 preventing marriage between Chinese or black men and white women. Chinese men found work as cooks, waiters, store clerks, or butchers in Chinatown, or as agricultural workers, laundrymen, or domestic servants outside.

In 1871 a Los Angeles mob killed twenty-one Chinese and looted the area where Chinese lived. In September 1885 twenty-eight Chinese were killed and fifteen were wounded in a riot in Rock Springs, Wyoming, when white coal miners refused to work with Chinese laborers. Also subjected to anti-Chinese agitation from the Workingman's party of the 1870s and the hysteria generated by an anti-Chinese press, which referred to them as "wily," "corrupt," "thieving," "murderous," "liars," "cunning," and "fiends," the Chinese defended themselves by organizing associations to serve as mediators between the Chinese-American and white communities. Some of the associations still exist in Oakland's Chinatown.

Frank Chin is one of a distinguished group of Chinese-American writers who lived at one time in Oakland's Chinatown. He said that the Chinese chose Chile and Mexico as destinations before arriving in California. When the Chinese arrived California was mostly inhabited by Mexicans, but by the late 1880s Chinese were as numerous as whites. So essential to commerce were the Chinese that Wells Fargo Bank printed an English/Chinese phrase book in order to foster communication. According to Chin, today's assimilated suburban Chinese-Americans are ashamed of their railroad-worker and proletariat beginnings and want to project the image of being middle class and white because, he says, they are Christian. "They want to leave Chinatown. They are proud not to know anything about Chinese history. Why do we call ourselves Chinese when we know nothing about Chinese history? Why not call ourselves Japanese, Korean, Vietnamese? We look at the Chinese stories as an infection, a disease." Chin believes that the railroad-building phase of Chinese-American history should be regarded as one of heroism rather than as a source of shame. Chin is particularly offended by the absence of any Chinese face in the famous photo celebrating the joining of the Union Pacific and the Central Pacific Railroads at Promontory in Utah on May 10, 1869.

Contrary to the popular image of Chinese-Americans as passive victims, the Chinese sometimes met violence with violence, Chin says. "But we don't hear about these

ISHMAEL REED

episodes because Chinese-Americans are afraid of creating a bad impression of the Chinese. We were proud that we could handle dynamite, that we could lay track better than the whites." Chin sometimes calls Chinese-Americans "the Uncle Toms of American ethnic groups."

At first, the Chinese came to America to seek their fortunes in the gold mines, but they encountered so much resistance from anti-immigrant sentiment among whites— who always had the numbers and the firepower to enforce their version of affirmative action, eliminating job competition from Mexican-Americans, African-Americans, and Native Americans through force—that they left the mines for cities and farms. In 1882 Congress passed the Chinese Exclusion Act as a boon to white workers. The law was not repealed until 1943. In 1913 the Alien Land Law made owning land impossible for a Chinese person. By constructing the Temescal and Lake Chabot Dams in 1874–1875, Chinese labor contributed to the building of Oakland.

JUNE 15

Hey, hey / the blues is all right.

I thought that I'd seen the best event that Oakland has to offer when I attended the carnival, but on June 15, Everett and Jones Barbecue, Grass Roots Entertainment, and Brothers Brewing Company do one better at the annual BBQ, Beer, and Blues Festival. Even the aching knees of the next morning, after standing for about three hours, are worth it. No one should miss this spectacle. For $10, I get to see D'Wayne Wiggins, formerly with Oakland's Tony Toni Tone and the first producer of Destiny's Child, fabled blues legend Little Milton, and the great Bobby Womack, whose stock may be down among the critics but who has a huge grassroots following. The crowd is mostly middle-aged with a bent toward expanded waistlines, and the predominate fashion color is red. Even some of the white girls wear red. In the middle of the scene, dancers wear black Stetsons while other people sport Afros, dreds, processes, and cornrows. I even spot someone in snakeskin pants. One middle-aged white man dances in a Hawaiian shirt. A whole lot of rockin' is going on. The B.B.A.B. has a picnic atmosphere. For a $20 ticket you can sit at a table, topped with red-and-white-checkered cloth, and from these VIP seats, enjoy your barbecued ribs and fish. The rest of us stand. We don't mind because most of us are dancing to the bands. I can't keep still. Little Milton is introduced and comes on in all black. I mean black hair, black shirt, and black pants with dark glasses. His deep crooning delights the ladies. Blues singers not only sing their songs, but impart some counseling along with them. Little Milton also includes an invitation to use black magic: "Sprinkle goofer dust all around your door."

He promises the women that he'll get the men to redeem themselves. For both Milton and Womack, men haven't been paying enough attention to women or loving them correctly for some time now. The women in the audience yell and even shriek their agreement. Milton advises the men to "say what you mean, and mean what you say" and the way he says it, it sounds like fresh advice. His group consists of three electric

guitars, a keyboard, and drums. Bobby Womack receives a
tumultuous welcome when he finally appears onstage. One
of his hosts, a woman who has spent about twenty minutes
entertaining the crowd before Womack appears, is ecstatic
about having ridden from the airport to the concert in a lim-
ousine with the singer, who wears a purple suit and a purple
cap. Accompanied by two saxophones, a keyboard, and two
guitars, he launches into some songs that have made him
famous, "Shananana" and "That's the Way I Feel About 'cha."
The crowd knows the lyrics and sings along. How many contemporary poets can make the same boast? A favorite line is
"If you think you're lonely now / wait until tonight, girl."
Milton and Womack sing about betraying and being
betrayed. Milton sings about being "shot from the saddle."
Womack bemoans the one man he gave "the shirt off my
back." Today he's giving more than that.

AUGUST 24

Today is the fifteenth annual Chinatown street festival, and I
can't think of a better way to spend a Saturday afternoon. As
Carla and I walk through Old Oakland and head toward
Chinatown I show off my newfound knowledge of the area
to Carla. At the festival rows upon rows of food stands and
booths sell products: jade charms, trinkets, bead bags, silk-
screened T-shirts, plastic rings, cellular phones. The corporate sponsors with their emblems are everywhere: Buick,
PacBell, New York Life, Alta Bates Hospital, Bank of America, Allstate, Western Union, and Budweiser. Safeway has a

trailer selling canned goods. A huge dummy Budweiser bottle looms over the food stands. As Cookie Wong, who's performing on the bandstand, says, the air is filled with the smell of teriyaki. She's performing with Magdalyo and the Kwock Quintet, consisting of herself on vocals and musicians playing alto and tenor sax, trumpet, flügelhorn, keyboard, and drums. Ms. Wong does "Fascinating Rhythm" and "I'll Remember April" in a style that resembles Ella Fitzgerald, Sarah Vaughan, and some of the cool white female singers of the 1950s. Mostly Ella.

I buy some chicken-on-a-stick and some Thai soup and we head down to a stage where a group from the Mahea Vehiyama Center for International Dance at Berkeley is performing. The leader is an Afro-Asian woman named Mahea. She says that Polynesian dance isn't meant for entertainment but is performed as an act of commemoration. Accompanied by drums, a group of young women perform beautiful hulas. On another stage an interracial group of teenagers called The D.P.G. Dance Group perform some hip-hop moves. Hip-hop keeps showing up at these city events, regardless of the ethnic emphasis. It's becoming the rice that goes with every meal.

AUGUST 31

Carla and I show up at 11:45 A.M. for the sixth annual gay pride celebration, officially billed as the Lesbian, Gay, Bisexual, Transgender, Intersex Pride Festival. At the moment there are tensions between the African-American and gay communities. Gays are viewed by some blacks as among the most aggressive regentrifiers, and even some gay blacks like Marlon Riggs and Barbara Smith have criticized gays for racist attitudes in their attempt to mainstream. Once a majority in San Francisco's Fillmore district, blacks blame their displacement there on white gays who have a stereotyped reputation for being great fixer-uppers. One gay man was quoted in a local newspaper as saying that instead of buying Cadillacs, blacks should put money into down payments on houses, as though blacks routinely had the same access to capital as he.

As we enter Frank Ogawa Plaza, a lesbian comedian is onstage telling toilet jokes. Among the performers are Cris Williamson, Lucie Blue Tremblay, Vicki Randle, Kindness, Rhythmix, Lady's Mem'fis, Duece, Once', and Over Our Heads. There are the usual booths, both for commercial and public service purposes. Carla and I agree that among those we've seen at events celebrating the 150th anniversary of the founding of Oakland, the audience attending this event is the most creative in its attire. Styles range from those of heavily made-up transgenders who carry boas to those dressed more informally but no less carefully coordinated. At the Homo Hop bandstand, located at Fourteenth Street and Clay, Carla and I sit in chairs behind two young white women sitting on the curb. One is wearing braids, chino pants, and black boots. Her white-and-pink pit bull is straining on a leash. Her friend is wearing a green T-shirt bearing the words HARLEY DAVIDSON MILWAUKEE. One man wears a baby-blue velour sweatsuit and matching cap, a fine homo hop ensemble.

The *2002 East Bay Pride Guide* excerpts a piece by writer Tim'm West on the gay hip-hop scene: "So often articles about gays in hip-hop either romanticize the spectacle of studs or homothugs listening to (presumed) straight hip-hop at secret clubs or an article about a suspect and closeted homosexual who is almost always quick to deny the gay rumor. When there is mention of gays and lesbians on the production end of the hip-hop industry, emcees, b-girls, and deejays are often passed off as not being popular or mainstream enough." The article goes on to name some prominent gay and lesbian hip-hop artists, many of whom are here today: Deep Dickollective, Hanifah Walidah Deadlee, Rainbow Flava, DJ Mister Maker, and Tori Fixx. The King of Hearts (drag kings), a troupe of women dancers dressed up like cowboys who amateurishly execute some steps made famous by Michael Jackson's choreographer, Michael Thomas, perform later. Unlike the crowd at the blues and Chinatown celebrations, this one seems subdued. At one point an emcee, disappointed after several attempts to rouse listeners, tries to provoke them by calling them boring but they remain unprovoked.

SEPTEMBER 2

None of the crowds we've seen at other events exhibits the joy and enthusiasm of those who attend blues performances. My purpose for attending Oakland's Art and Soul Weekend is to hear poetry, but I never get to the reading. First I pause at the gospel stage where three robust women belt out some tunes. One repeats the line "He will / Yes, I know he will." Ron Stewart of the Blues Society has told me to come over to the gospel stage, sandwiched between the federal and state buildings, and given me a list of the performers: The Passions, Beverly Stoval, Country Pete & His Cottonfield Blues Band, Freddie Hughes, Little Frankie Lee, Jimmy McCracklin, Jesse James, and Natural Four. I then make my way to the center of Civic Center. In front of the fountain some of the area's leading blues performers perform on a bandstand. Brueghel, who painted *The Kermess,* would have enjoyed this scene. A dancing man balances a beer bottle on his head. A youngster with Down's syndrome dances during every number. Frankie Lee, "The Trickster's Son," performs. Ron Stewart introduced me to Lee at the noon concert at Frank Ogawa Plaza a few days ago. He's hitting one of the popular themes of the blues now, the lament of the abandoned lover. "Went way down to Miami, Florida / Couldn't find her."

The call-and-response aspect of the blues fuses a connection between the audience and a performer, based on shared experience. "Anybody here know what I'm talking about?" At one point the singer starts to preach. In the African tradition of literature it's okay to give advice, to let people know how the artist feels about an issue. "Trouble with the world today is that there are too many people trying to love too many people at one time." Jimmy McCracklin appears. He's been introduced to me as a Hall of Famer. He is dark-skinned with jet black straight hair, and wears a black linen suit, white shirt, and white tie. I think of Gede, the gangster trickster who has migrated from Haiti to Miami and Brooklyn. McCracklin editorializes about the younger black audience who nowadays are stuck in a one-track hip-hop mode. "White people know more about the blues than black folks," he says. His blues orchestra consists of a baritone sax, a tenor sax, a trumpet, drums, and a bass guitar played by a white musician.

His singer's name is Sweet Nectar. After the white musician takes a solo, McCracklin looks on approvingly and says to the mostly black audience, "Let's give it to him." McCracklin sings a song that is a blues reply to a young person who asked him to do a Michael Jackson number. He then gets down to business with a song about suffering. "For forty days and nights you made me suffer before you called me back on the telephone." Before breaking into one of legendary Jimmy Reed's standards, McCracklin says that he promised the late Reed that wherever McCracklin went he would sing Reed's trademark song. A teacher from Kenya and her students recognize me standing near the bandstand, taking notes. They come over and introduce themselves. One of the students, Watin Kaire from Kikuyu, Kenya, says that her father, Kimotho Kaire, an ex–Mau Mau, loved the blues.

November 15

Tennessee and I meet writer William Wong, a former classmate of Frank Chin's, in front of DeLauers, Oakland's famous all-night newsstand on Broadway and Fourteenth Street. Wong, an author, journalist, and former commenta-

tor for the *News Hour with Jim Lehrer,* later tells us that
Broadway was once the dividing line between Chinatown
and the rest of Oakland, but Chinatown now spills over into
Old Oakland, despite the initial objections of the redevel-
opers who discouraged Chinatown businesses from moving
across Broadway. He is modestly dressed in a hooded sweat-
shirt, jeans, and sneakers. We begin our tour at the site of a
failure. The building that now occupies the space at Eleventh
and Broadway was to be Hong Kong U.S.A., a sixty- to
eighty-story building that would be partially funded by a
Hong Kong investor. After an investigative reporter traveled
to Hong Kong and discovered that the investor's credentials
were suspect, the project was abandoned. This was not the
first or last redevelopment deal to go sour. The space is now
occupied by the Trans Pacific Center.

In the 1950s, according to Wong, Chinatown was dying,
but a resurgence occurred when the immigration laws were
changed in the 1960s, abolishing quotas. As a result of the
change in the law, immigrants arrived from Taiwan, Korea,
the Philippines, and Southeast Asia. Some of those from
Taiwan, Hong Kong, and Southeast Asia, like the late U.C.
Berkeley chancellor Chang-Lin Tien, came to the United
States for education. Others were hi-tech workers headed
for Silicon Valley. Now, Wong estimates that the Asian-
American population of Oakland is 15 to 17 percent, while
the black population has declined from 47 percent in the
1980s to 35 percent today. The Hispanic population has
grown from 13 percent in 1990 to 22 percent in 2000.
We walk to Pacific Plaza, a four-block, Hong Kong–style

development at 988 Franklin that includes restaurants, retail stores, housing units, a cultural center, and a library. One walks through a corridor to an open square where Asian-Americans of all generations are milling about. Some elderly men are seated, talking.

Wong says that geopolitics shaped Chinatown. He provides Tennessee and me with the history of Chinatown and the events abroad that formed it: the occupation of China by the Western imperialist powers in the 1840s, which lasted for a hundred years, and the war between China and Japan, during which the Chinese Nationalists and Chinese Communists forged an alliance with the United States only to engage in a civil war after World War II ended. After the defeat of the Nationalists led by Chiang Kai-shek, Chiang and his followers fled to Taiwan. Wong describes how the hatred of communism by successive generations of American politicians led to an embargo on goods from China, but how, following détente with China during the administration of Richard Nixon, goods from China began pouring into the United States. Wong points out that some vegetables like dry mushrooms would not have been available to Chinatown residents in the old days.

Wong discusses how land use has evolved over the generations. When he was growing up in the thirties and forties, there were gas stations, hardware stores, and barbershops. For example, located at Eighth and Franklin is a street sign that reads BILL LOUIE'S CORNER, site of a former gas station that Louie sold in the eighties. An old brick building located at 703 Franklin has a sign in the window, ONG ASSOCIATES.

Wong says that he attended a Chinese school with the Ongs, who also own the seventy-year-old building at 708 Franklin where, the following week, Legendary Palace, a Chinese dim-sum restaurant and banquet facility with five hundred seats, opens. The building was formerly used as a nightclub, a garment factory, a bookstore, and a rooming house. Almost $3 million was spent to retrofit and rehabilitate the building into an 11,500-square-foot restaurant featuring dishes of twelve chefs from Hong Kong and China. The building was often the scene of a struggle between Chinatown social activists who wanted to preserve it for housing for the poor and elderly and those who desired its use for commercial interests. Chinatown's version of the clash happening all over Oakland. It is the classic California conflict. In this case the commercial interests won out.

Wong remembers with fondness George Katombu's barbershop, which was located at 372 Seventh Street. He got his haircuts here. So did the black mayor Lionel Wilson. Across the street is the Salvation Army. Wong says there have been fears among Chinatown residents about the clientele to which the Salvation Army caters, as well as a few muggings. At 723 Webster is the site of the Wong family's former restaurant, Great China.

The Cathay Bank sits on the former site of a restaurant owned by the family of Ben Fong-Torres, the writer and editor for *Rolling Stone* magazine. The Chinese school that both Wong and writer Frank Chin attended was located at Eleventh and Harrison. As a result of the civil rights movement that broke barriers that had kept them below

Broadway, many of Frank and Bill's generation were able to leave Chinatown and intermarriage became more common. The hip-hop generation has extended the trend toward biracial and interethnic relationships.

I always wonder why opponents of diversity always single out blacks when discussing "multiculturalism," "cultural relativism," and "political correctness." At about the same time as my tour of Chinatown with William Wong, Juan Gonzalez, a *New York Daily News* correspondent, and William McGowan, author of a book about diversity ruining American journalism, held a debate broadcast over C-Span. Most of McGowan's anger was directed at blacks, even though "diversity" includes Latino, Asian-American, and Native American journalists as well as blacks. When Todd Gitlin complained about the protest waged by parents against textbooks used in Oakland schools, which they deemed exclusive, he singled out black parents, even though Chinese-Americans and Jewish Americans also complained—rightly so—about the content of the books. And the more I gather testimonies from Asian-Americans, Native Americans, Latinos, and even Euro-Americans about the impact of the civil rights movement on their lives, the clearer this idea of a black leadership role becomes. Even those cultural phenomena that were apparently aimed exclusively at blacks, like Kwanzaa, now include whites. At least in Oakland.

Black Cowboys and Gold Diggers

GEORGE ROTHMAN and his neighbors have made the news. He is suing them over their objection to his having black friends as guests in his home. The harassment of his black visitors began ten years ago when Ed Dillard, president of the Black Chamber of Commerce, visited him. One neighbor reportedly said that he didn't want any "Jews or niggers" on the block. When Tennessee and I arrive on his street, we get the once-over from his neighbors. Rothman doesn't take it lying down. "Racism is a cancer and I've been fighting it all of my life." George Rothman is not black.

Born in 1916 in Brooklyn, he grew up in a Jewish neighborhood and didn't see a black person till he was twelve. When he was still a kid an incident had a profound influence upon Rothman's thinking. He saw ten white guys beating a black man. He tried to interrupt the beating. "The man is bleeding; why don't you leave him alone?" Rothman pleaded, but the whites told him to mind his own business.

The injustice of ten white people beating one black led Rothman into the struggle.

Later he worked on 116th Street in Harlem, where he met local luminaries like Father Divine, but Rothman was impressed by only one person in his life: Malcolm X. They discussed racism on the corner of 116th and Lenox in the 1960s; Rothman was the only white person Malcolm invited into the mosque. Rothman worked at the time as general organizer for the department store union, organizing strikes against department stores on behalf of their employees. According to Rothman, organizing women in the 1930s was difficult because they were considered "second workers," and because they were afraid. He organized against May's department store but was fired after the negotiation of a contract; the head of the union called Rothman in and announced that he had to let Rothman go because he belonged to the union's left wing.

Rothman never finished college but went to the Asia Society on Seventy-seventh Street to study Asian culture. He attended for three years. Rothman says that he is still interested in all cultures and is an avid history buff. He came to Oakland in 1966 and, while selling black encyclopedias, ten volumes dealing with black culture and history, met black activists. The idea for a black cowboy parade began to take shape.

George Rothman says that the Black Cowboy Parade might be Oakland's oldest ongoing parade. It began when the Oakland Museum's ethnic guild, organized to improve the museum, felt that too few blacks were involved in the museum's programming. Rothman had never heard of black cowboys until 1975, but after the guild did their research they discovered that four out of ten cowboys in the Old West were black. At the time, Rothman was also involved with a group called the Oakland Traders, people—black, white, and Hispanic—who came together to promote Oakland. The Traders began a sister-city program and the first city selected was Accra, Ghana. Many Traders were community activists and black small-business owners at a time when it was very hard for black businesses because of redlining. Rothman was also the director of Blacks Unified to Motivate Progress (BUMP), a group organized by Booker Emery and Ralph Williams—both "mayors" of West Oakland, the largely black district. Somehow a New York Jew became director of a black organization.

In 1975 BUMP formed the Black Cowboy Association. *Bazile* Black councilmen Wilson Riles Jr. and Leo Bazile were supportive, but others were against it. (The most the parade has ever received from the city was $8,000.) The BCA contacted black-owned ranches in the Bay Area and in Tracy, California. The ranches cooperated. The group publicized the event and people who could ride horses showed up. The Oakland celebration was modeled after the Calgary Stampede, where the city closes down for ten days and everything becomes cowboy. In 1986 the queen of the Calgary Stampede was a black lady. The Black Cowboy Association invited her to become their guest and she accepted and came to Oakland for the parade.

OCTOBER

At the annual Black Cowboy Parade, attendance is up over the previous year. With high school and ROTC bands playing and executing march tunes and drills, this parade has a more military bent. The most polished marchers are those from the Oakland Military Academy, a pet project of the mayor's. Their drills are supervised by two women, one white and one black, attired in camouflage outfits. Critics have accused the mayor's military academy of diverting funds from public schools. As Tennessee and I take photos, we are approached by a black man who asks us where the Black Indian Association is supposed to show up. He said that one of his ancestors was Choctaw. Cowboys and Indians, together at last.

A RALLYING SONG FOR THE
GOLD DIGGERS

To the mines! to the mines! away to the mines,
Where the virgin gold in the crevice shines!
Where the shale and the slate and the quartz enfold,
In their stony arms the glittering gold.
'Tis in vain that ye seek any longer to hide
Your treasures of gold in your rivers so wide,
In your gulches so deep, or your wild canyon home,
For the Anglo-American race is come.

The Californios fought valiantly against this encroachment, but were no match for development-hungry hordes pouring in from all over the world to stake claims. Governor Pico, the black Mexican governor, summed up the feelings of the Californios at the coming of the '49ers, an attitude of dismay mixed with admiration.

We find ourselves threatened by hoards of Yankee immigrants who have already begun to flock into our country, and whose progress we cannot arrest. Already have the wagons of that perfidious people scaled the most inaccessible summits of the Sierra Nevada, crossed the entire continent, and penetrated the fruitful valley of the Sacramento. What that astonishing people wants I cannot say, but whatever enterprise they embark they will be sure to be successful. Already these adventurous voyagers, spreading themselves over a country that seems to suit their tasks, are cultivating farms, establishing vineyards, erecting sawmills, sawing lumber, and doing a thousand other things that seem natural to them.

One elderly Native American recorded by Joaquin Miller shared Pico's sentiments: "The whites were as the ocean, strong and aggressive; while the red men were as the sand, silent, helpless, tossed about, run upon, and swallowed up." Writer Hugo Reid described the '49ers as ". . . vagabonds from every quarter of the globe. Scoundrels from nowhere, rascals from Oregon, pickpockets from New York . . . assassins manufactured in Hell for the expressed purpose of converting highways and byways into the theatres of blood. . . ."

I ask Malcolm Margolin, an expert on Native American culture in the region, whether visible sites have been left behind. The next day, November 30, 2002, the kind of coincidence occurs that seems to happen whenever I'm writing a book: A story appears on the front page of the *Oakland Tribune* about a demonstration in which Native Americans complained about a new shopping mall that was built upon a shellmound that Margolin mentioned. Carla and I go down to Bay Street in Emeryville and find streets crowded with new shops: Victoria's Secret, Williams-Sonoma, Banana Republic, and Old Navy. We locate the Barnes & Noble towers, where the demonstration took place. No Indians. I take a picture of a scene that clearly demonstrates the source of the struggle between developers and preservationists: construction equipment digging into ground that holds the bones of Native Americans. "How would you like it if someone built a shopping mall above Arlington Cemetery?" a demonstrator asked. Bin Laden has complained about American armed forces being located near the sacred sites of Islam. How would we like Arab armies around Saint Patrick's Cathedral? Maybe many Arabs hate us because we don't take the time to consider their feelings about these sorts of things. We're too high on progress. One commentator says that the Americans couldn't reach the same kind of accommodation with the Native Americans that the Californios had established because they were in too much of a hurry. Nothing's changed.

In his book *The Age of Gold* H. W. Brands writes, "In the
aftermath of the Gold Rush, a new American dream was
born—the enduring conviction that sudden wealth was
potentially within everyone's grasp." This is the dream that
unites the '49ers with the '99ers, the crack rushers with the
gold rushers. Introduced to the Oakland streets in the mid-
eighties, crack afforded black youngsters the ability to make
sums of money beyond the dreams of their forefathers who
worked in the service and manufacturing industries. Just as
violence attended the wildcat capitalism of the gold rushers,
the crack rush has taken its toll on the young black people
of Oakland. Malcolm Margolin quotes author Jim Holiday,
who said that the Gold Rush was the first time that sudden
wealth was there for the plucking, that you could just go
and grab wealth. You didn't have to earn it. You didn't have
to accumulate it; you didn't have to have good character.
You just had to take it.

NOVEMBER 28

On Thanksgiving, Carla, Tennessee, and I drive to my half
brother Michael's house in the Montclair hills, an affluent
district represented by a retiring councilman, Dick Sprees,
for dinner. Michael has invited about thirty people of different generations to join in on the feast. Some are members of
his wife Denise's family. Denise helps Michael run his pedi-
atrician practice; all of the children of Oakland are members of his extended family. Their ranch-style home looks
out over the city and is built to get the full treatment of a

day's sunlight. It is a Calfornia home. Michael's house is so high in the Montclair hills that radio towers I see on my walks around Lake Merritt are near it.

Before we dine everybody around the tables joins hands and is led in prayer. Denise's father has just died and she asks him to join us from heaven where, she says, he is probably having a beer, or maybe a glass of gin. Both Denise and Michael have faced the good times and bad times with style and grace.

The men and Tennessee are gathered watching football. They have an assistant coach's knowledge of basketball and football. I'm impressed. They're also computer whizzes and talk about what you need to download the latest movies. They mention Eminem's *8 Mile* and *The Great Greek Wedding* (or something like that). Thousands of black professionals are gathered around dinner tables and TV sets this Thanksgiving, but you seldom see them in the press. That same week I watch Steven Spielberg's miniseries *Taken,* in which the black men are scientists, generals, med students in contrast to some of his former movies, in which black men are depicted as dregs; here they are compassionate and idealistic, and even the black heavy, the general whose attitude is rough and abrasive, can be excused for his rudeness on the grounds that he's just doing his duty. But such depictions of black men are rare. Just as the white underclass is hidden from the public, showing up from time to time on places like the *Jerry Springer Show,* the black upper class is kept out of sight, lest some white Americans lose their self-esteem, whose foundation is the myth of black inferiority, their psychological Prozac.

DECEMBER 2

Tonight, I attend a party thrown by the 100 Black Men at the Oakland Convention Center at which Michael is to be honored. I and a few others show up without the requisite black tie, but otherwise, the room is decked out. Business professionals and political leaders are there, including Don Perata, the new state senate majority leader. Earlier in the day, Michael and my other half brother, Kip, who could be my twin, showed up at the house. I teased them about Thanksgiving. Their maternal grandfather is a full-blooded Indian who grew up on a reservation. I ask them how, with their Algonquin heritage, they could celebrate a day that represents the betrayal of the Indians, who, after showing the colonists how to survive a New England winter, were slaughtered by their new friends. And they weren't the only Indians who would be betrayed.

DECEMBER 5

Calvin Simmons was the black conductor of the Oakland Symphony, and after his death the Oakland Auditorium's opera house became the Calvin Simmons Theatre. Annalee Allen made a potent observation when she remarked that some of the black movers and shakers of Oakland had died young. Housing an arena, opera house, art gallery, and banquet rooms, the building opened in August 1915. According to a writer for the Oakland Artscape in 1987, "its unique back-to-back stages separated by a steel curtain became a model for similar buildings across the country." Woodrow Wilson made a presidential address in the arena and Anna Pavlova and Nijinsky performed in the opera house. New chandeliers were added in 1927, and in 1958 the opera house was remodeled. In 1982, to commemorate the hundredth anniversary of Kaiser's birth, the complex of which it was a part was renamed the Henry J. Kaiser Convention Center. Later that year the opera house was named the Calvin Simmons Theatre and in 1984 it received a new roof, floors, seating, and carpeting. Tennessee and I find ourselves sitting under the theater's molded roof, painted ornaments, and gold leaf.

In 2001 we attended the Kwanzaa marketplace at the Oakland Convention Center, housed in the Marriott Hotel. Today we await the beginning of a Kwanzaa concert and performance. Tennessee and I are among a handful of adults attending this concert. About five hundred schoolchildren have poured out of school buses and streamed into the theater. The show begins when Elly Pardo Farcia, a white woman dressed in traditional Yoruba attire, steps out and begins to drill the students on the seven principles of Kwanzaa. They know them and what they stand for: *Umoja* (unity), *Kujichagulia* (self-determination), *Ujima* (collective work), *Ujammaa* (supporting black businesses), *Nia* (purpose), *Kuumba* (creativity), and *Imani* (faith). These are students who are deemed backward and incorrigible by the education establishment, but this demonstration proves once again that black students will learn if the material is interesting and, with the growing number of alternative sources of information like festivals such as these and the Internet, they are also learning to detect the myths and plain lies that pass for a humanities education in the United States.

When the drumming starts the audience whoops it up. The performance begins with the pouring of libations in honor of the ancestors and to celebrate a good harvest or marriage. Next the masked figure, the *egunegun,* dances to ward off bad spirits. The drummers are led by Pope Flyne. Other performers are Lee Puma on congas and flute and a dance group from Castlemont High School, who perform traditional African dances under the direction of Razaki Aladoky, a master of the talking drums from Nigeria.

After Kwanzaa, we have a Victorian Christmas with our fellow tenants of Preservation Park. Entering through the black-iron gates of Preservation Park is like being transported to another time, and we are dazzled by the Christmas lights arrayed against the Victorian, Stick, Italianate, and Gothic-style houses. More important, the buffet consists of marinated mushrooms, spring rolls, soft cheeses, shrimp and vegetables, steamed vegetables with dip, spicy meatballs, spicy shrimp, fruit tart cookies, and strawberry cheesecake. Ted Lacey says that he hasn't heard any more about the city selling Preservation Park. Denise says she's going to Bahia for a well-earned vacation. The tenants are busy in conversation. I recognize some new faces.

DECEMBER 12

I held my office hours yesterday and so today I'm lying in bed reading Joaquin Miller's book *Life Amongst the Modocs.* It's as interesting as Twain's work, but Miller might be considered a traitor to his race. Not only does he often take the Indians' side against the white men, but he had a child, Calle Shasta, by a Native American woman, Sutat. And he defended the Indians when they massacred some white settlers, on the grounds that white men had raped Indian women, which was a sport not only among the Spanish and the mission priests but among the gold rushers as well. Though California Indians are usually depicted as primitives scrounging around for acorns, the Modocs were not to be messed with. The Modocs held off the American army for six months under their chief, Kientpoos, or Captain Jack. One of those who was in on the kill once the American army broke through was Jefferson Davis. His role as an Indian fighter and his presidency of a slaveholding "country" marks him as a most ignominious character, even for American history. Miller reminds us that craven development has been a problem ever since the Indians were relieved of their stewardship of the land.

Game and fish have their seasons to come and go, as regular as flowers. Now the game go to the hills, now to the valleys, to winter, to have their loves, to bring forth their young. You break in upon their habits by pushing settlements here and there. With the fish you do the same by building dams and driving steamboats, and you break the whole machinery of their lives and stop their increase. Then the Indians must starve, or push over onto the hunting and fishing grounds of another tribe. This makes war. The result is they fight—fight like dogs! Almost like Christians.

Miller's book was published in 1873, about twenty-four years after the beginning of the Gold Rush. By coincidence, today's *Oakland Tribune* reports another victory for the developers and commercial interests as the Brown 10K juggernaut rolls over another neighborhood group. The Jack London neighborhood residents, after opposing the building of a pair of high-rise housing projects—"one possibly 18 stories high"—settles with the city, which paves the way for the high-rises to be built. The *Tribune* notes that the settlement opens the door "for tall buildings being erected in other sections of the city. Traditionally, high-rises have been relegated to downtown."

DECEMBER 14

Today we go to the Peralta House for a Christmas party. Some Hispanic children are dressed in the style of the Californios. There are some black kids there, too, all wearing zany hats designed by a man calling himself the King of the Universe who sits at a table patiently making hats, presumably a good job for the King of the Universe.

Then Pomo Indians accompanied by some Navajos begin a dance. Dance is essential to the Native Americans of California. In one Pomo story, a Pomo leaves the land of the dead after being told by his deceased sister not to follow her there. The dead had been having a ball, though, dancing, so when the Pomo returns home he and other members of the tribe dance for four days. The leader at today's party is Lanny Pinolu, who began dancing when he was five years old and

learned the feather dances from his mother and grandmother. He says that "dance is inside of you; it has to be
brought out." His father was a Pomo, his mother a Miwok.
These dances, Pinolu claims, are ten thousand years old. The
men wear shorts covered with the feathers of red-tailed
hawks. These feathers are also a part of their headwear. The
men are barefoot and shirtless. The women are fully clothed.
Unlike in American modern dance, these dancers come in
all physical shapes. "If a child wants to dance, the spirit
comes to them," we are told. The program begins with the
dancers and singers performing a prayer song for the creator.
California Indians don't use drums. A flutelike object made
of elderberry wood, split in the middle, is used as a clapper
stick. Pinolu asks the audience to join in and instructs them
to dance "as though you were running down the street."
During an interview after the performance, he tells me that
the dances are based upon the movements of deer and
eagles. After the performance, I join the guests, who continue to file into the kitchen for plates of *buñuelos,* tortillas
topped with honey, and wonder whether California had
been better off under the eagle deity than the god of wild
capitalism that the invaders brought.

Mansions and Bullets

RINGING LAKE MERRITT are buildings of architectural interest: the Scottish Rite Temple, the Alameda County Courthouse, the Veterans Memorial Theater, the Peacock building at 2122 Lakeshore Drive where poets Victor Cruz and Nancy Mercado once lived, and a highrise luxury apartment building at 1200 Lakeshore where Huey Newton once lived. At the intersection of Grand Lake and Lakeshore stands the Grand Lake Theater, an old California movie palace that was lovingly restored down to its five-thousand-lightbulb marquee. The stateliest of all is the Camron-Stanford House.

Paul Duchscherer and Douglas Keister's book *Victorian Glory* describes the mansion.

> *This elegant Italianate house remains a representative of the numerous mansions once strung along the curving shore of Lake Merritt. It was originally built for Will and Alice*

Camron, who subsequently rented the house between 1878 and 1881 to David Hewes, a grading and paving contractor in San Francisco, who used the house for many social functions. Later on the house was purchased by Josiah Stanford (the brother of the San Francisco railroad baron Leland Stanford), who would live there for twenty-one years. In 1906 the city of Oakland bought the Camron-Stanford house for the newly organized Oakland Public Museum, which opened in 1910 under the curatorial leadership of Charles P. Whitcomb. The house was vacated when the new Oakland Museum of California was built nearby in 1967.

From Elizabeth Way, who conducts tours of the house, we get more details, such as the fact that Will Camron and Abraham Lincoln were friends. They both worked for the father of Mary Rutledge, who was a romantic interest of Lincoln's. Way also clarifies that the Hewes family owned the house from 1878 to 1883.

Rich families of Oakland like the Heweses and the Stanfords turned their homes into museums that included items acquired on two-year grand tours of Europe and the Middle East that many families took as part of their education. As a museum the Camron-Stanford House includes fifty-two cases exhibiting items from early New England life: foot warmers, weavings, knives, forks, and an old saw that resembles a bicycle. Miniature replicas of these displays have been sent to schools throughout the district. There are also exhibits of stuffed animals like armadillos and quails. Their ethnographic collections are extensive. The museum once imported a Hopi Indian to teach the making of kachina dolls. Part of the tour is a presentation of an Academy Award–winning film about the house and its part in Oakland history, *Living in a House;* its narrative was culled from the voices of the women who lived there. While Ignacio de la Fuente first saw Oakland as "a diamond in the rough," for the rich in 1876 Oakland was "a second Venice." An influx of two hundred thousand refugees from San Francisco after the 1906 earthquake changed that. The stately houses were subdivided. It was this Oakland that Gertrude Stein, daughter of a wealthy family, had in mind when she made her remark, "There's no there there."

The preservationists blame the modernist Stanfords for undoing the work of Hewes, who left the house after he and his wife, who had a chronic pulmonary disease, moved to southern California. Because the Stanfords favored modernism, those staples of Victorianism were thrown away and had to be recovered or reproduced when the house was saved by preservationists. Oakland's Junior League did the research that led to the house's being restored, using such sources as Hewes's granddaughter Charlotte's diary. Craftsmen were brought in to work on the cut glass and chandeliers, to plaster, and to wallpaper. In the upstairs parlor are French clocks, a reproduction of the Sphinx, a rug bought in Constantinople, a Chickering piano, and photos of family members framed in lockets. The highlight of the home's history was a visit from the Hayes family, President Rutherford and his wife, Lucy. Five hundred people attended the reception held in their honor and the silver punch bowl is still on display. During the restoration, items of historic worth were brought from other locations. Dr. Samuel Merritt's marble fireplace was donated to the preservationists. In another parlor stands a Christmas tree decorated in the manner of the Victorians; toys were not gift wrapped in those days. The father would simply present the presents. In another parlor are buffalo chairs containing buffalo tusks. This was Hewes's way of drawing attention to the slaughter of 3 million buffalo as a result of railroads owned by Crocker, Hopkins, Huntington, and Stanford.

DECEMBER 17

Rain again. Carla, Tennessee, and I drive to the Pardee Mansion, which stands across the street from Preservation Park. We walk out into traffic because construction of a new condominium has blocked the sidewalk. David A. Nicolia greets us at the entrance of the house, which takes up a half a block between Eleventh and Twelfth Streets. Our tour is supposed to last one hour, but because I am covering the house for this book, Nicoli is kind enough to double the time.

This house, representing a key period in Oakland's history, was nearly demolished to make way for a freeway. Nicola gives us some background.

The Pardee sisters and the people of the First Unitarian Church made sure that the freeway stopped one block west of where it was supposed to. I think they wanted to demolish the coach house, which was built from 1868 to 1869.

The Pardees had migrated from France to England to New Haven, Connecticut. Enoch was born in Rochester, New York. First he went to the Midwest and later arrived in San Francisco. He went up to Yuba City to the mines for a year. He told his wife, Mary, that once he hit his goal of five thousand dollars he was going back to Ohio, but he fell in love with California. The air was better, so his health improved. He established himself as an eye doctor on Clay Street in San Francisco. He arranged an escort so that Mary could come. They moved to Oakland because Mary got tuberculosis and the weather was sunnier and warmer. They moved in December of 1869 and Mary died a year later. George, their son, was twelve.

Enoch was elected mayor of Oakland. George graduated from Oakland High School and went to the University of California. George followed in his father's footsteps and they practiced ophthalmology together in San Francisco. Then the college's campus moved from Oakland to Berkeley. It used to be located on the site of the parking lot at Franklin and Fourteenth. People tore down historic buildings in those days. They wanted more modern buildings. The Old City Hall was torn down to make way for the fifth City Hall, the current City Hall. After the earthquake of 1906 they tore it down. The third City Hall had just been built when it was burned down during the anti-Chinese riots of 1877. It might have been an act of arson. Pardee declared martial law.

Both Enoch and George served as mayors of Oakland. George was elected mayor in 1893 and governor in 1902. He was a Republican and a lot of black men supported him *and gave him the margin of victory. He won by three thousand votes and his votes from black men (women couldn't vote in those days) came to eight thousand. He wouldn't have won if it wasn't for them. He didn't give them what they felt was their share of patronage and the black men protested.*

The Pardees had a lot of money. Enoch had made fifteen thousand dollars in the mines, a fortune in those days. They were property owners. They were very dedicated political reformers and conservationists. The water that was supplied by private companies was overpriced and very unsanitary. They served on the Public Health Commission and led the fight for the establishment of East Bay MUD, which was voted on by the citizens of Oakland in 1907. George provided the leadership that led to this measure being adopted.

The Pardees didn't maintain an elaborate lifestyle and they didn't entertain a lot of famous people. They were environmentalists. Theodore Roosevelt was George's role model.

In one room of the house there is a photo of John Muir, Theodore Roosevelt, and George Pardee together.

Enoch caused some gossip when, at the age of fifty, he married a twenty-six-year-old high school teacher in Lodi named Emily. They had a daughter named Eleanor who died of typhoid fever. George, his son, was upset about the difference in ages and, at the wedding reception, refused her hand. When Enoch died, she came into a lot of money. She spent seven years traveling around the world and landed in Baltimore. We talk more about Mary than Emily, but, in some ways, Emily was more interesting. Emily was a suffragette and a founder of the First Unitarian Church and the Women's Club after returning to Palo Alto, but couldn't shake the rumor that she was a gold digger who married Enoch because of his money. She and George were locked in a suit over the house that was settled in 1897. Emily got the furniture, George got the house.

George moved his family into his house. The furniture came with George and his wife. The family lived in this house until 1981. George had a wife named Helen, whom he met in high school, and daughters Florence, Madeline, Carol, and Helen. They lost two of their daughters, Florence and Carol, through tragic accidents. Helen and Madeline lived here until old age. They occupied the house until 1981.

We at the Pardee museum have no desire to do a nine-teenth-century home. We want to show the changes that were made over the years. Helen traveled to Central and South America and to the South Seas. She traveled some in the United States, but she didn't travel that much. In general, these objects were brought to her as gifts. She was a collector. One knew not to come to the Pardee house on a Sunday afternoon without bringing something to Helen. Helen liked to collect candleholders, lighting devices, and tea services. She collected stuff from non-Western cultures a lot, even though she had stuff from the eastern United States and Europe. She also collected Jewish stuff. The Pardees weren't Jewish. They weren't religious. George never stepped into a church. We have an obligation to decorate the house for Christmas, but Christmas was not a big deal in the house. He didn't want

Christmas trees because he was a conservationist. He dyed turkey feathers green to invoke the holiday.

My first paid work was to dust the furniture eight hours a week. I hated it. It was not safe for the furniture, either. Over here on the Christmas tree are ornaments. Miniature replicas of the state of California, reproductions of the ballots used to elect George governor, and miniature top hats to invoke the memory of the inaugural ball.

The house was built of redwood from the Oakland hills that was processed at Dr. Samuel Merritt's sawmill. The family spent most of their time in the rear parlor. They had a radio and a record player and one of the first wireless remote controls. They couldn't climb the stairs anymore because of their age, so they had to give up their upstairs bedrooms. This family had a lot of tragedy and sadness.

They had a Chinese gardener, chauffeur, and cook. The Pardees had a black housekeeper named Marian Malone who held the house together. She lived in an apartment in the rear. There were two old people in the front, while there were parties, exclusively black, in the back. The most valuable object in the house is a chandelier from a famous photographer of Yosemite. He was as famous as Ansel Adams. His name was Carlton Walkman.

The furniture in the dining room is mostly Germanic. The guy who owned the furniture was a spy for Germany and forced to leave the country after World War I and so Pardee got the furniture around 1920 for about two hundred dollars. [We leave the ground floor for the upstairs bedrooms.]

The money for upkeep comes from private funds, not from

the city of Oakland. The city wants to spend money on more modern buildings. This is the bedroom. The bed was mahogany and the sheets were from China. Over here is Madeline and Helen's bed. Madeline kept a journal of boyfriends and evaluated them. Here is the playroom with a red-tailed hawk and an Indian pot. [Carla, who has finished a book called Rediscovering America, *for which she did research on Native American art, identifies the pot as Acoma. We are all impressed.]*

Back here is the billiard room, with a shark-tooth sword from Africa. These baskets are from Africa. Helen stole these human skulls from a church in Guatemala. [We go out into the backyard, stepping over rain puddles.]

The house is meant to look like a country estate. The water tower provided water to the house. When they got new plumbing they had to get a second water tank. Back here is the coach house. There are horse stables. They had a Norwegian groom. The room he stayed in was hot in the summer, cold in the winter, and smelled like horse manure.

There is something poignant about touring a house where two sisters, survivors of celebrations and tragedies, lived until 1981. In the old Oakland you might have acquired wealth and objects from all over the world, but your children and wives died early; no amount of money could buy off tuberculosis, diphtheria, and typhoid. The image of the stolen skulls remains with me days later, when I show up for the Black Panther tour. It could be called the Black Panther Death tour. David Hilliard, a survivor of the war between the Black Panthers and the F.B.I. (assisted by the local police), speaks with emotion about his numerous, pointlessly dead comrades.

DECEMBER 21

Some grad students from San Francisco State, mostly Asian-American and Chicano, board the tour bus. Four men wearing turbans arrive in a beige Jaguar. Hilliard stands at the front of the bus and addresses the group through a microphone. He wears a shirt bearing the photo of Huey Newton in a butterfly chair.

> *This tour is about education. This is about when Oakland was in the middle of a political struggle. So I would expect that you give me the kind of attention you give your teachers or professors. After all, this is an educational tour. Let me qualify myself. I am David Hilliard, one of the founders of the Black Panther party. I was the Black Panther party's chief of staff and the party's administrator while Huey Newton was in prison and Eldridge Cleaver was in exile. I met Huey Newton right here in Oakland in 1953. We went to elementary school and junior high school together. We played in this park right here. [He points out of the window to De Fremery Park, the site of the picnic.]*
>
> *I came here from the South to West Oakland when I was eleven years old, so that is a brief description of my qualifications to be a historian of the Black Panther party. This is a very important description of the Black Panther party, if you*

are doing research. The history that I talk about is the history that I made. I was the founder of the children's program and the free health-care program. All of these programs that are on your list—I was a major part of. So what you are getting here is primary information from people who made the history. Bobby Seale and I are the oldest party leaders still alive. Huey Newton was the founder (the minister of defense), Bobby Seale second in rank (the chairman), Eldridge Cleaver the minister of information, and I the chief of staff. For those of you who are doing serious information on the Black Panther party, your primary research should direct itself toward Huey Newton, who has a new book out called The Huey P. Newton Reader.

When people write about our party they reduce us to some cultural nationalist movement. This is not true. We were a revolutionary and political movement. This book talks about this truth. It is very important. He talks about women and environmental issues. The anthology was commissioned by Toni Morrison and has Huey Newton's writings in it. Huey Newton did his dissertation on the FBI's war against the Panthers. It is in the anthology. Some of our articles are here. We also have Black Panther T-shirts, records, and speeches. I want you guys to ask questions, because this is a classroom.

You guys don't have these types of civil rights movement now so you need this history. We have this crazy man taking us to war, a return to segregation with Trent Lott, police repression, homelessness, wars; these are really bad times. You need this history. The Black Panther party's philosophy is to distribute the wealth of the United States to everyone. Our phi-

Blues City

losophy was power to the people. This is a dull period compared to the sixties. This tour is depressing, because twenty-eight of the members were murdered. It is very painful to relive these memories.

[The bus arrives at Eighteenth and Chestnut, where Hilliard met Malcolm X for the first time.] One day I saw this guy coming by wearing glasses, with a star and a moon on his cap. I saw Malcolm X. I met Malcolm right on this corner. I thought that he was a Mason. I saw him on TV and I said, "There he is, the guy on the corner." I wanted to be like Malcolm. Huey Newton and I were influenced by Malcolm X. [The bus heads up Market Street.] Every one of these stores was owned by African-Americans. We have a hard time finding stores like this now. I suggest in five years you will see that the African-American population in Oakland will be nonexistent under Jerry Brown's plan.

Forty percent of Americans identified with the Black Panthers. We ended in 1970 because of the government. The FBI wanted us to be gone. To this day we are still seen as criminals. This tour is about our side of the story. Revolution is not legal. Most of these progressive organizations are against revolution. These people shouldn't call themselves "progressives." There is nothing revolutionary about that. You have to be careful about these groups. If you start a revolution, you expect to go to prison.

Hilliard points to a traffic signal located at the corner of Market and Fifty-fifth Streets. After some black schoolchildren were injured or killed in 1967 at this intersection, which motorists still speed through as though engaged in a stock car race, members of the party formed an armed guard for the children and escorted them across the street. The motorists began to respect the guard. The Oakland City Council had informed the party that a traffic signal wouldn't be erected until 1968, but, impressed by the Panthers' determination, the council erected a signal much earlier, on August 1, 1967. Located at the same intersection was formerly the Office of Economic Development Corporation (now the Ebony Lady Salon). Here at 5500 Market (the corner of Market and Fifty-fifth Streets), party philosopher Huey Newton wrote the famous Ten Point Program. Hilliard then points to the home of Bobby Hutton at 898 Fifty-sixth Street at Market.

We are now heading towards Bobby Hutton's house. He was fourteen when he joined the Panthers. Martin Luther King and Malcolm were in their thirties. We were the youth of the movement. I raised the money to write articles from our point of view. Today you have a special treat. Bobby Seale is in town and he's going to talk to you. I called him and asked him. He's coming on the bus for about forty-five minutes. This is the cofounder of the Black Panther party. Do you have any questions? [He is asked about a group calling themselves the new Black Panther party.]

These new Black Panther party members have taken our image and are just using our name. They are Muslims. There is nothing wrong with that, but they use our name. They came out of [Louis] Farrakhan's movement. They take our move-

ment and confuse it with the Pan-African Movement and anti-Semitism. They wave guns and try to fight with the Klan. But we fought the police and the FBI. It was a racist department. There were only two black men on the police force in Oakland during the 1960s. These new guys have distorted who we are. They have no programs or agenda. Our name is not a name to trample over. They misuse our history and they have nothing in common with us. If you study our history you would know that.

Black people in this country helped create Asian-American studies and Middle Eastern studies. No one else was doing this but us. We ought to be connected that way. We had chapters with Native Americans, Chinese, Japanese, and Australians. We helped America become the multicultural country that it is. We helped shape those landscapes. It didn't just happen overnight. Therefore you shouldn't isolate yourselves from the black students whose population has been reduced considerably after Proposition 209.

Proposition 209 ended California admissions policies that assisted Asian-Americans, Hispanics, and African-Americans. It also reduced the number of women faculty. Hilliard continues, "I challenge the African-American students to clean this mess up and to claim their history."

The bus rolls up Fifty-sixth Street and pauses in front of Bobby Seale's house. Hilliard hops down from the bus and enters the house. He exits momentarily and reboards the bus. He tells the disappointed students that Seale waited for them but had some other business to attend to and had to leave. Merritt College, where Seale and Newton organized the Panthers, is up the street on Martin Luther King Jr. Way. Preservationists saved the building from demolition. Hilliard says that ethnic studies began at Merritt College, which is now a building used by senior citizens. Hilliard says that Jerry Brown had promised him that a Black Panther museum would be located in the building but reneged on the promise.

"We are going to our first office," he announces. We get out and enter the All Good Bakery located at 5624 Martin Luther King Jr. Way. The salespeople are busy trying to sell baked goods while we tromp around. Some of the students begin purchasing goods. On the wall are news clippings that mention the Panther tour in the *New York Times* and a Japanese newspaper. There are also photos of Hilliard and Jerry Brown campaigning together in happier days. Hilliard says that it was here that Newton, while watching a rally in China, got the idea for buying Mao's "little red books" wholesale and selling them to students at the University of California campus. On another wall are photos of stars who are fans of the bakery, Chris Rock and Patti LaBelle among them.

We travel to at least fifty campuses a year to tell our side of the story because the FBI has reduced us to criminals and drug dealers. It has nothing to do with politics. I don't know if the students know what is going on in Iraq. A few years ago they didn't know how to spell Iraq. *They talk about how they hate Saddam Hussein and they don't know who he is.*

*So the fact of the matter is that we live in an unconscious era.
It is totally apolitical and ahistorical. African-American students should fight to learn this history. It is about students
fighting for control over curriculum. The Panthers were about
that. Seventy students were killed at Jackson State and sev-
enty-eight at Georgia State. The civil rights movement
was reduced to Martin Luther King. He died back in 1968.
Back then the Panthers were the number one political organization. We were more powerful than King. Students identified
with us.*

*The liquor store we boycotted was here. [He points to a
building on 5624 Martin Luther King Jr. Way.] We boycotted
it because it wouldn't make contributions to our Breakfast for
Youth program. The guys from Yemen own the liquor stores
and I know this because I got their support. [David Hilliard
ran for city council in 2002.] I wanted them to know that
there were other ways to make money. The people we boycotted had asked us to get them a license for cognac. We boycotted the distributors until they decided to do business with
the black liquor stores. After this victory we asked them to give
us food to be distributed to the needy. They said that they'd
give us five hundred dollars. We insisted on food. They
refused. We closed down their stores. We negotiated with them.
We finally had all of these black businessmen sit down at a
table and decide that they were going to support the community. This is what made us more powerful than most groups
imaginable. Jerry Brown is doing exactly what he wants to do
because most of his critics protest and move on. The Panthers
don't do that. People like to dog the Panthers because they*

can't stand up to us. If you look at the survival programs, I would say that eight out of those ten programs are as relevant today as they were back then. The universal health care, education, racial profiling, police oppression, and all of that stuff. Our program empowered all oppressed people. [The bus rolls down West Street. Hilliard's former residence at 4722 West displays a FOR SALE sign.] There is my house. We [Hilliard and Newton] walked to school together, Woodrow Wilson School [now Carter Middle School]. [The bus passes 4419 Martin Luther King Jr. Way.] This was a first meeting place where this hat store is. The cops shot at us through the window. [The shooting took place after Huey Newton was acquitted for the murder of Officer Frey.] They got two weeks' suspension without pay. They said they shot at us because they were handling a demonstration and they were suffering from fatigue at U.C. Berkeley and so they were letting out steam. They were the first drive-by shooters.

[The bus arrives at the former site of Saint Augustine Church (now Saint Andrew's Baptist Church), located at 2624 West Street.] Saint Augustine Church is where we started our Breakfast for Children program. We had thousands of people in the church. It became a national program. A lot of black people back East didn't know Oakland existed. They knew L.A. and San Francisco. When they found out about us, they knew only that about Oakland. I want you students to go down to City Hall to the city council and tell them to bring things back to Oakland that are reminders of the Black Panther party. This is California history. If you go back East or even out of the country, the people are proud of us. Lionel

Wilson, the first black mayor, won because of the Black Panther party. Bobby Seale was the first person to overturn a one-hundred-and-ten-year-old rule by Republicans. The highest voter turnout in the city was when Bobby Seale ran for mayor. Lionel worked with us. That's why he got elected. We demanded that the police who work in our community had to live there as well. We called for a residency requirement and to put more women and more minorities on the police force. They had recruited white men from the South to be on the police force. They were white racists and they came from outside the city.

Today we have to deal with racial profiling at the airport, if we look a certain way and have a certain name; they tap our phone and e-mail and they want to fight wars in the Middle East. That's fascism. In 1967 and '68 we started fighting against this and 9/11 has started a new McCarthyism era. We need to study the history. The suffering never really stopped. The right is much better off than we are. They have a lot of power. We organized the prisoners. George Jackson was part of our prison movement. Saint Augustine was where his funeral was held and thousands attended. The prison movement began with Huey Newton's arrest.

Huey Newton was put in the prison because he allegedly shot a police officer. Ever since 1968 we'd had meetings about organizing an antifascist movement. On the fourth of April we met at Saint Augustine and the police arrived. We chased the police officers out. They came back with more and the monsignor of a church. We called Bobby Seale and Augustine's pastor slammed the door in the police officers' faces. That night

Bobby Seale got a death threat from the White Citizen's Council.

That same night Martin Luther King got shot. So we went among the community trying to stop any riots that might take place. We prevented the kind of rioting that took place in other cities. That evening we had our guns and we were riding around in vans.

There are bullet holes on this house over here. [He's pointing to another West Oakland home.] It was between my house and Bobby's house. This was the location of an hour-and-a-half gun battle. This was a shooting that went on. There were helicopters. The police were banging on the door to get in. A lot of those people that were there I never saw again. I still wonder how the police knew we had those guns. About a third of the Panthers were informers. They wanted to shoot up the house and ignite it like they burned those people up in their house. [Hilliard is referring to the standoff between the Los Angeles police and the Symbionese Liberation Army that ended in the incineration of some SLA members.]

That night Eldridge Cleaver took off his clothes in the pitch black to show he wasn't hiding any weapons, and good thing he did. Bobby Hutton didn't remove his clothes and so they shot him even though he had his hands up. They didn't shoot me. I pretended I didn't know the Panthers. I just said that I was in the house because I was scared the police would shoot at me. I said that I was Robert Johnson, the son of the lady whose house I'd run into. They took me down to the police station. I was nervous. It was eleven o'clock. These were two white police officers and they were racist as hell. When they found out who I was they beat me. A black officer recognized me and made them stop.

In 1969 Bobby Seale got kidnapped and shot. This was in Chicago at a convention. Cleaver left the party for Cuba. I became the leader. This was the most repressive area. Coming back from Algiers I was arrested because of a speech I made that was later alleged to have threatened the life of President Nixon. I was in prison for four years. Nixon resigned the year I was released. They didn't have a case. The last year in prison, I was asked by the FBI to work for them. I didn't want to. The reason I was finally released was because the Panthers were almost nonexistent. We ended with Huey Newton's death in 1989. He had become a drug addict and a dealer. During that whole period we celebrated drugs. Every corner had a liquor store. A lot of people smoked blunts and they didn't think anything was wrong with that. Bobby Seale had a drug addiction that was continuous. Drugs and alcohol were self-medication. They fixed you.

Here is where Huey Newton got killed. Here is the stencil on the ground. Huey Newton had a gun and had drugs. He got killed so this guy [the murderer] could be a big shot among drug dealers. This guy is serving thirty-six to life. There are still drugs going on. If you want to see the change in Oakland, come here. Don't go to City Hall. The government had something to do with it because they took away after-school programs. The politicians have given up. We're going to head back.

The tour ends near some West Oakland street corners where people are openly dealing drugs. Hilliard's voice quivers at times when he recounts the painful history of the Panthers, but at other times it becomes strong as he talks about the Panthers' accomplishments. Accomplishments that the city has failed to acknowledge. If they can name a road and a park for Joaquin Miller, Confederate sympathizer, white supremacist, horse thief, and jail breaker, a man who joined an assault on Native Americans; if they can name half the institutions in Oakland after Jack London, a thief and a mugger; if they can name a city after Frémont, under whose Bear Flag Republic Californios were murdered, held incommunicado for months, and had their land stolen; if they can name a street after Andrew Jackson, who, according to Ward Churchill's *A Little Matter of Genocide,* "supervised the mutilation of 800 or more Creek Indian corpses—the bodies of men, women and children . . . ," then certainly they can identify landmarks related to Huey Newton, who organized a group that brought black power and international attention to Oakland.

DECEMBER 24

Today I drive a few blocks to Marcus Books, another Oakland landmark. I read that a map titled *Walk Oakland! Map & Guide* has been published to highlight Oakland's "historic walkways, neighborhoods, and landmarks, to raise awareness and encourage appreciation of Oakland's many great places." The store is packed, even though the latest draw on talk shows is the anti-intellectual attitudes of Afro-Americans. I suppose that the people who push that line don't frequent black bookstores. Blanche Richardson, the store's owner, eyes me. I ask her about the map and get three.

The next day, Christmas, Carla and I drive up to the Woodminster Amphitheatre, located at Joaquin Miller and Sanborn Roads. Dedicated to the writers of California on March 5, 1941, the theater features spectacular WPA-style art. On each side of cascading waterfalls, friezes depict figures engaged in artistic creation, painting, sculpting, and writing. We walk down the steps leading from the waterfalls, the scent of plants and trees available to us, and come upon a small, oval-shaped pool in the middle of which gushes a fountain. From this vantage point we look out upon the skyscrapers of Oakland and the bay beyond. In 1955 the pool was dedicated to Gertrude Mott as a tribute to her contributions to the civic life of Oakland. We drove farther down Joaquin Miller Road to Joaquin Miller Abbey, the house where Miller wrote his poem "Columbus." It's boarded up now, but a Joaquin Miller website shows it as it appeared when Joaquin Miller lived there, surrounded by trees.

DECEMBER 27

Writers for the *San Francisco Chronicle* and the *East Bay Express* point to some of the problems facing the Brown adminstration. Kara Platoni writes in the December 25 *East Bay Express:* "It also became painfully obvious that the downtown is lacking the 10,000 new residents that Brown hoped would be lured there." Chip Johnson writes in the December edition of the *Chronicle:* "The city is facing a 3 percent deficit this year and a 5 percent shortfall next year. It all adds up to painful cuts, dwindling resources, and trouble." On the same page my eye catches an event that's taking place at the Lawrence Hall of Science: *A '49er's Life with the Miwok.* "Program on Sierra Miwok depicting the Gold Rush era from an American Indian perspective." It's taking place on Saturday. I decide to go because Lanny Pinolu said that his mother was a Miwok. While preparing a mailing for the post office, I'm listening to a discussion on *Talk Back Live.* Ann Coulter has attacked Kwanza as some kind of celebration of hate. A young man who is presented as the editor of Africana.com, a Time Life product, defends Kwanza but refers to its founder, Maluana Karenga, as "a fossil." When I reach the post office, I notice some Kwanza stamps, but I'm told that they are all sold out. I buy some stamps that address the issue of breast cancer.

Saturday. The rains continue. Carla and Tennessee have an appointment to have lunch with Timothy, my oldest daughter, but Timothy has spent the night with her boyfriend and cancels out. I drive up Grizzly Peak Boulevard to the Lawrence Hall of Science. The newspaper didn't say that the program was actually a play to be performed for kids. I'm surrounded in the auditorium by parents and their children. The play is called *Friendly Fire,* and is performed by one actor, who is part of a group called Duende, which performs plays with California themes. Dressed in Gold Rush attire—brown boots, jeans, brown shirt, and miner's hat—the actor is in character as James Blake, addressing some folks in his hometown, giving the reasons why he's returning to California. He talks about how he and some other men from the town set out for California, traveling from Mexico to San Francisco by ship in sixteen days. After some time in San Francisco, "a sinful city," they move on to a mining town called Jamestown. Then to Sonora camp, where there are some fancy-dressing Peruvian and Mexican women. At Sullivan Creek they encounter Indians selling venison and fish in exchange for whiskey and blankets. The party decides to push off into Indian country and comes upon some six naked Indians who are mining gold. They trade them a barrel of whiskey for some buckskin. A member of the party named Bill decides to murder the Indians on the grounds that "when civilization comes, Indians have to go." They slaughter the Indians with Kentucky rifles and dispose of their bodies. The scene is so gruesome that Blake, who has participated in the massacre, gets sick. They return to their camp with twenty nuggets of stolen gold and began roasting venison and drinking whiskey to "celebrate." Blake is separated from his companions and, after a fall, awakes to find himself surrounded by Indians. They carry him to their village, attend to his injuries, and feed him. He becomes comfortable with the Indians, learning their language and enjoying himself, when an Indian runner, someone who traveled from village to village with Indian news, arrives in the village. The runner identifies Blake as being among those white men who murdered six Indians. Led by the father, whom Blake has decided to call Laughing Fox because of the Miwok prohibition against using real names (revealing one's name opens it to being stolen), the Indians debate what to do. The father says that the Indians are at fault for their deaths because they were from the north and had been pestering his people with their quests for gold. Moreover, they have violated a cardinal principle that one shouldn't take things that can't be replaced, a principle that shows the difference between Miwok philosophy and that of the gold miners. For the father, "the white man will be caught in his own landslide." (His isn't the only Native American prophecy that foretells the destruction of white America.) The father is the spokesperson for the tribe, as well as the one who announces breakfast and assigns the day's duties to the men and women. Blake, the narrator, pays tribute to the Miwok for their attitudes toward nature. Their way of handling fire to help replenish the forests explains the name of the play, *Friendly Fire*.

A scene in which Blake joins an Indian hunting party praises the Miwok attitude toward animals. When the party encounters a grizzly bear, Laughing Fox negotiates with the bear; in exchange for a fish, the bear allows the party to pass. One of the women asks Fox the nature of his conversation with the bear. "Oh," Fox says. "He warned us that a bad winter was approaching."

Fox decides that Blake should marry one of his relatives. Blake meets the girl and a wedding is arranged. There is a call for a great feast, and Indians travel to the site of the wedding, bringing fruit and meat, some walking for three days. They are entertained by Indian clowns, whose faces are painted white. Blake marvels at how the Miwok have taken him in as one of their own, even though he was involved in the murder of Indians. After whites invade a neighboring Indian village and take over the land, the homeless refugees arrive and have to be taken in. During winter the whites kill hundreds of deer, the Indian food supply, "without letting their souls free," which was the Miwok custom when killing a deer. The whites invade Blake's village and murder the parents of his bride. He encourages Laughing Fox and Fox's father, Thundering Crow, to complain to the Indian commission, but they are ambushed by some whites, who knock Blake unconscious.

When he awakes, he finds himself face-to-face with white men who want to know what he's doing hanging out with savages. "You haven't gone native on us have you?" one asks. When he tries to tell them the truth, they dismiss his explanations as stemming from his delirium. He doesn't know the fate of Laughing Fox or Thundering Crow. He does learn the fate of his companions who participated in the murder of the Indians. Three have drowned; another was killed in a knife fight over a Mexican woman; and Bill, who encouraged the deed, has fled with the gold. The play ends with Blake explaining to the people of his hometown that he has to return to California and find out the fate of his Indian companions, even though it might mean that he has to be a man between two worlds. He has become, in a sense, a white Indian.

After the performance the actor answers questions from the audience. He says that the play was based upon true stories, the playwright drawing the script from journals and diaries, some of which were written in Spanish and some of which came to light only fifty years ago. What struck the actor, he says, was how bizarrely the invaders portrayed the Indians. We still view those who are different from us as being bizarre. But the means for dealing with them has become more sophisticated.

In addition to the Lawrence Hall of Science, another institution bears the name of Lawrence: Lawrence Livermore National Laboratory. Its role, according to a profile in the *East Bay Express,* has been that of steward over the nuclear stockpile. We've come a long way from Kentucky rifles.

DECEMBER 29

In Oakland the favorite choice of weapon is the Saturday night special. Sometimes they're used on Friday nights. On December 27 Oakland got its 109th and 110th homicide victims. At fourteen, Keith M. Harris is the youngest. His cousin Jerry Duckworth was twenty-four. They were partying when a gunman shot at least a dozen bullets through their front door on Campbell Street. Though most of these homicides are drug-related, some are the result of random or mistaken identity. Today, Sunday, December 29, the *San Francisco Chonicle* displays the photos of the year's homicide victims. Many of them were on parole, having done time for drug crimes. I always think of the movie *Welcome to Hard Times,* based upon a book by E. L. Doctorow in which townspeople must face an outlaw who returns annually to terrorize them. The same thing happens when parolees are discharged from prisons. They return to the inner-city neighborhoods to commit auto burglaries, larceny, break-ins, and assaults. The *Wall Street Journal* once ran a story about how those who had the least to fear from crime, sub-urbanites, were the ones driving the primacy of law enforcement as a political issue because of the fear invoked by images on television of black criminals. Politicians take advantage of this fear and demand that preventive or reha-bilitative programs be cut. For example, Pell Grants for pris-oners, which made up only 1 percent of the national education budget, were eliminated in Bill Clinton's Omnibus Crime Bill (although the black upper classes sup-ported Clinton, more blacks were incarcerated under his administration than ever before in history). And so while the suburbanites might achieve a cheap thrill from their politicians' legislating mandatory minimum sentences, the results of such harsh programs are felt in urban neighbor-hoods, not theirs. When he was governor Jerry Brown pro-posed indeterminate sentencing as a solution to the rising murder rate in Oakland, a measure that was eventually rejected as racist. Under that plan, convicts would not have been released from prison until they furthered their educa-tion or learned a trade. But given the racist and sometimes fiendish practices of the criminal justice system (e.g., in one California prison, Pelican Bay, guards encouraged prisoners to engage in gladiatorial fights, sometimes with fatal results), there was no reason to believe that such a system would not have been open to abuses.

David Hilliard says that the new Oakland criminals are illiterate and dangerous. Crack, minimum/maximum sentencing, and the welfare reform bill, in addition to the get-tough policies adopted by nearby San Francisco and Berkeley against the homeless, most of whom are veterans and black men and most of whom have a work history, further strain Oakland's resources. According to a report from Pacifica's KPFA, the police in Berkeley were cracking down on the homeless, while on January 14, 2003, Berkeley became the first city in California, and only the seventh in the nation, to issue a proclamation that farm animals have feelings and deserve to be protected, which gives the impression that Berkeley's city council cares more about the feelings of chickens than about those of the African-American veterans and others who are living on the streets of that same city. Not to be outdone, San Francisco voters passed a measure that would supply the poor with vouchers and only $59 per month to live on. The measure passed even in San Francisco's liberal districts. Advocates for the poor said that the homeless would now drift toward Oakland as the last city with any sort of compassion. It's the city, after all, that welcomed two hundred thousand refugees from the San Francisco earthquake of 1906.

JANUARY 1, 2003

We begin the new year with a photo of the Shorenstein building on the front page of the *Oakland Tribune*. I don't see any difference between this glassy tower and some of the others that have shot up downtown. But the caption accompanying this building indicates more problems ahead for the beleaguered city, where black men are shooting each other like ducks in an arcade. Because of the collapse of the dot-com economy, upon which the Brown administration pinned its hopes, the building is only 31 percent occupied. The writers of the piece term Oakland's problems "intractable" and quote a speaker for the grassroots group ACORN: "The housing situation is bad. The schools are terrible. There's not enough jobs. The crime rate is higher—all those murders. The city just doesn't have the answers." Nonetheless, two controversial projects are going ahead: the Leon Quarry housing project, which has been opposed by neighborhood groups, and the Forest City project, which is being subsidized by the city at the tune of $60 million. Developers of both have ties to East Bay politicians, including Jerry Brown, who has received money from the developers. Even in the lavish rooms of the showpiece mansions that have been restored to replicate their nineteenth-century preciousness, evidence of Oakland's intractable problems shows. Elizabeth Way, who led us on a tour of the Camron-Stanford mansion, said that one day while she was hanging Christmas lights in the sun deck, somebody took a shot at her. The bullet hole is still there.

JANUARY 24

Though many Oakland Hispanics live in poverty, their occupation of the Fruitvale district has led to the rise of brown economic power, with an attendant broadening of a brown middle class, even as the sections of Oakland where the residents are predominately black are desolate and abandoned.

But the contributions of browns to the culture of Oakland aren't purely economic. While awaiting the beginning of a Kwanza ceremony at the Kaiser Center in December, Tennessee and I visited the Oakland Museum, where a show entitled "Arte Latino: Treasures from the Smithsonian American Art Museum" was up. I was impressed and decided to return later for a closer look. On January 24, Carla and I return to the museum with Eloisa Hall, my barber and a close family friend. A sparkling, vivacious grandmother, Eloisa lives with her husband, Robert, in a hacienda-style home in the Oakland hills. She was born in Nicaragua and came to the United States when she was eighteen. We had decided to attend the show together during a Christmas party held at her home (the Halls' display of figures and lights is the most spectacular in the neighborhood).

The Hispanic artists represented in the show work with a number of materials and address a variety of themes, many of them Christian. Some of the artists are Catholic and others combine Catholic and West African religion—a synthesis that goes by the name of "African Spiritism" in the show's catalog. One piece, called *Farm Worker's Altar*, created by Chicano artist Emanuel Martinez, celebrates the worker's cause, even including clusters of grapes to symbolize the fruit that was boycotted by many Latinos. On one side of the altar a woman holds corn in one hand and grapes in the other. Inside of the sun, which appears over her head, is the mestizo tripartite head, which symbolizes the mixed heritage of the migrant workers. On another side of the altar is a brown-skinned Christ, which conjures a number of immediate associations, but sometimes it's risky to give a superficial reading of Christian symbols when they're used by artists belonging to non-Western cultures. One day earlier in the year I attended a luncheon in honor of Long Standing Bear, chief of the Blackfeet Nation, held at Moose's restaurant in San Francisco, that city's "in" place for the establishment (that same day Senator Diane Feinstein was dining on the first floor). Saheen Little Feather was wearing a cross, which prompted someone to ask whether she was Catholic. Much to everyone's surprise she answered that for her, the cross was not a symbol of Christianity, but represented the four cardinal points.

While some of the exhibits feature realistic portraits, others combine different materials in order to create a collage. Maria-Canas's *Totem Negro XVI* is composed of fragments of "ancient manuscripts, postage stamps, geographic forms, pre-Columbian temples, and maps." Another grab bag of objects forms *El Chandelier* by Pepon Osorio; according to the catalog, the hanging chandelier holds "swags of pearls and mass-produced miniature toys and objects, including palm trees, soccer balls, Afro-Caribbean saints, cars, dominoes, black and white babies, giraffes, and monkeys." Amalia Mesa-Bainsalso uses found objects in her *An Ofenda for Dolores del Rio,* an altar that resembles those you can find walking through the Fruitvale district on the Day of the Dead. This particular altar was dedicated to Dolores del Rio, the Mexican film star. The installation included "perfume bottles, an open fan, and jewelry [juxtaposed] with Mexican and Chicano bric-a-brac, linking personal effects with cultural symbols." Angel

Rodriguez-Diaz's contribution to the show was a portrait of Sandra Cisneros, author of *The House on Mango Street*. "She is dressed in a black Mexican dress that is decorated with sequins and embroidery, and holds a patterned *rebozo* (shawl) that snakes around her bejeweled arms." While some of the work uses symbolism and abstract themes, Frank Romero's *Death of Ruben Salazar* is unapologetically political, created in honor of Salazar, a writer for the *Los Angeles Times* who was killed when he was struck in the head by a tear-gas canister that Los Angeles County sheriff deputies had fired into the Silver Dollar Bar. Just as powerful is *Man on Fire* by Luis Jiminez, in which "fiery red-orange flames engulf the monumental figure of Cuautemoc, the courageous young ruler who led the Aztecs in revolt against the Spanish conquistadores in the early 1500s."

After we view the show, we go to the museum's restaurant. We ask a man who is talking to another man behind the counter whether there is coffee available. Silence and a smirk from both men. This Brazilian man behind the counter had been rude to Tennessee and me when we visited the restaurant weeks before, but appeared to be doing handstands for the white women during the lunch hour. Grinning and carrying on. I'd just experienced the human experience at its highest only to be reminded of the human experience at its dumbest. I also wonder whether this man knew that without the militancy of Oakland blacks he wouldn't even have his job.

One artist whose work appears in the Smithsonian show is Rupert Garcia, probably the best-known Mexican-American artist in northern California. A stocky, powerful-looking man, he has a broad face, a heavy mustache, and a receding hairline. A few days after attending the exhibit, we meet him for lunch and he tells us his California story.

I was born outside of Stockton. I spent twenty-one years there. I loved it. To me it was great. I lived on the South Side, where working-class blacks, Latinos, and Asians lived. It wasn't a farm, but it was rural, outside of the city limits. I had to go to the bathroom in the septic tank. I started making objects when I was really young. My mom tutored me in how to draw. (I used to make "wishdrawings"—drawings of girls I wanted to be with.) People in my family were very creative. They were artists and dancers and they designed clothes. My two brothers studied piano. I was never discouraged about being poor and being an artist because my mother paints. And she is absolutely amazing. She's eighty-two.

I also got my artistic impulse from my grandmother in Jalostohtlán, Mexico. It was magical. Many years later I went there. Tia Juana, my great-aunt, makes clay figurines. I saw this and couldn't believe it. She was the water woman of the town. My cousins in Guadalajara make jewelry, but my brothers and sisters here do not draw or paint. The education system told them that their art was stupid and that discouraged them. In California the schools told me that being modern means to disconnect from your culture.

Someone told me that I wouldn't make any money being an artist. It was the white guy who met my mom and married her. I hated him from the moment he stepped into the house.

I had no idea why I use strong color in my art, but I do.

I am attracted to it. Color meant a lot to me when I was little. I wasn't into politics, but I felt the segregation in Stockton. The town was based upon apartheid. When you leave one part of Stockton, you feel the divide. I didn't have a word to understand why it was this way. The sixties saved my life. I went to junior college in my hometown—called Delta College—and then I went into the air force. After that I came to San Francisco to become an artist because I had been into Jack Kerouac in high school and I knew that the Beats and San Francisco had to do with rebellion. I was twenty-one when I moved to San Francisco and I lived in the Haight on Cole. I didn't know how to become an artist. I didn't know where the good galleries were in the city. But I felt like every gallery I saw was the Louvre because it was in San Francisco.

I came to Oakland in 1981. Oakland had a house that we could afford. We wanted to stay in San Francisco. We used to live near the Oakland Zoo and we lived there for ten years. We needed a bigger space. Now we live in Adams Point. The top is the studio and the second floor has the bedrooms and the libraries. It was built in 1917 and we thought it was a Julia Morgan [a prominent Bay Area architect in the early twentieth century], but I called the history room at the library and they told me it wasn't. We still love the house.

I don't prefer to be called Hispanic, Chicano, or Indigenous; I just prefer whatever term will make me money. I first called myself Mexican, then American, then Mexican-American, and then Chicano. I am not a nationalist like some artists are. I am evolved in my own work. I found my voice in the 1960s. I have my own life, and that's the way it goes. I no longer have a group association. My aunt got me into politics when we went to see César Chávez. The first subconscious political piece I did was in 1967, about Vietnam. I was in the air force and was starting to be exposed to what was going on. But I only did two drawings in Vietnam; I was more concerned about staying alive. I was asked by the sergeant of my squad to do drawings and I said no. I didn't want to do work on behalf of the military. When I was in Montana I was doing duty at a post in the Rockies. It was a beautiful day. I started drawing, and the sergeant caught me. He looked at my drawing, tore it up, and threw it in the garbage can. I told him that he couldn't do that. Later on I said, "You're an idiot, Rupert. You are such an idiot. He could have done anything to you." But he just walked away. He never said a word.

Despite its lack of literary reputation, from the days of Jack London till today, Oakland has been the home of many distinguished writers, including the Wongs—Nellie, Shawn, and William—Frank Chin, Maya Angelou, Anne Rice, and Stan Rice. Another writer who uses Oakland as a setting is American Book Award winner and detective novelist Lucha Corpi. Tennessee and I met her at a popular gathering place for poets and artists, the Coffee Mill, and heard her Mexican-American story, a complementary tale to Rupert's story.

My grandfather was Italian, from somewhere near Florence. My grandmother was Hispanic, and she had some Native American blood. On my mother's side the name is

Constantino. My father's mother was three-fourths Mexican. She had a dark complexion. One of my brothers was dark with black hair and black eyes. One had green eyes and blond hair. All of my other siblings were somewhere in between.

I had no idea that I was going to be a teacher. I wanted to be an astronomer. My father was a telegraph worker. He was a big believer in education. He felt that the educator of a family was the woman. I remember my family insisted that all of us get an education. I had six sisters and two brothers. My older brother and I started school together when I was four; we lived in a small village and he didn't want to go alone. He wanted to take me everywhere with him. My father explained this to the principal and the teacher. It was agreed that I would sit in the back of the classroom at a desk. But I learned everything.

I came to Berkeley in 1964, when I was nineteen. My family comes from the southern part of Veracruz in central Mexico. I moved from there to Berkeley where my husband was a professor at U.C. Berkeley. I lived there for ten years. I got an education there. We lived on Dwight and Dana and on Ashby near the Telegraph COOP . . . all over the place. Then in 1970 I moved to Oakland, a half a block from the border of Oakland and Berkeley, near the White House Liquor Store. Now I live near Mills College, close to Fruitvale. Oakland is so special. First of all, there are eighty major languages spoken here, and people of every color and humanity. There is no neighborhood in Oakland that isn't integrated. Oakland is a special city with special problems.

I teach adult education and ESL at Cleveland Park School. The school is good, but the district is in bad shape. The *thing is that injustice always brings about some sort of violence. We can't blame the school and the teachers for kids' dropping out. The curriculum is not as relevant as it used to be. We have to begin to give the kids the survival skills they need.*

I started writing by accident. I started as a short story writer. In 1969 I started writing right after a divorce. I had no friends and no family here. All of my family is in Mexico. I started writing poetry. Being divorced with a young child, I had some decisions to make. I had to go back to school, graduate, and get a job. I had a job all throughout college. I don't think I chose to write, but writing changed me. I figured out that I had to make time to write. I didn't call myself a poet. My first publication was in a Norton anthology. Then I had work appear in an anthology with the work of a couple of Mexicans. I expect that my writing in Spanish limits the number of people that read my books. I write to please myself first.

When you talk about Latino and Chicano literature there are many varieties. People like me write short stories in English and poems in Spanish, while others mix the two languages. Some writers only write in English because they have no knowledge of Spanish. There are different variations of Spanish. You have New Mexico Spanish, Arizona Spanish. There is a writer who has lived in Arizona all of his life. His name is Miguel Mendez. He writes all of his works in Spanish. Mexicans could never accept him, but now he gets recognition, thirty years later. Mexicans usually never accept Chicano writers. People like me have lived in the United States for most of their lives. I go see my mother and brothers in Mexico. My ties to Mexico are very strong, but Mexicans

*say that I am too Chicana. I am too Mexican for Chicanos,
and for gringos I don't exist. I am in limbo. Prejudice comes
from ignorance. If people have never read our work, how can
they judge? I have been to conferences where both Chicana
and Mexican writers have participated. The issues are language, and then they talk about things that modern Mexicans
don't want to deal with, like the native history, the fact that
there is racism in Mexico. If you have dark skin and money,
you are accepted anywhere. However, access to opportunities
are slim. That is racism. They can't see that. I saw the same
thing in Brazil when I went to Bahia. The Portuguese
descendants feel that there is no racism in Brazil. They don't
accept that they deny people access to certain institutions. They
say, "Oh, you are talking about all of that history." I have a
friend who is from Mexico City. In my last mystery, there is a
character who feels that she is a reincarnation of Malencha.
When he read it, he said, "Oh, you Chicanas, why don't you
leave it alone?" I can't believe I have been here almost forty
years.*

The Killing Comes to My
Neighborhood . . . Again

CARLA AND I went to Honolulu to help promote *New
and Collected Poems* by Kathryn Takara by joining the
author at a reading at Barnes & Noble. We stayed at a hotel
in the center of Waikiki. We'd have our breakfast on the
patio at the Hilton across the street and some of the elderly
white tourists, seeing me and Carla, would scope out the
patio from inside before coming out for breakfast. There
was an orange alert that weekend so I guess they thought
that I was Al Qaeda. Tourism was down and the Americans
there seemed to cluster along the beach in front of the
hotel, which is how they act all over the world. Reluctant to
mix with the locals. We had a great last night in Hawaii,
during which I gorged on some Chinese food with Carla,
Kathryn, Harvey, her husband, and Kathryn's friends. When

I returned home, it dawned on me why Oakland really is Blues City. The killing that was breaking out all over town, even threatening people's safety in the tony Oakland hills, had come to my neighborhood again.

I had talked to the victim hundreds of times. He lived toward the Market Street end of Fifty-third Street in one of two motel-like structures located across the street from each other. He was a handsome, elderly black man who usually stood in the driveway next to his room when he wasn't walking through the neighborhood. He'd had a serious operation and lost a lot of weight, and the walking seemed to help his recovery. Tennessee told us of his death as soon as we entered the house. Later, Mary Lucas, the neighborhood historian, added the odd detail that on the day of the killing, there were so many black cars on the street that you'd have thought a funeral was taking place. He had been murdered by his son, just as he had murdered one of his sons. The police called it self-defense, and the judge ruled that the son be sent for psychiatric observation. A week later, he was back in the neighborhood. A neighborhood that, like many neighborhoods in the flats and increasingly even in the safety of the white sections, has seen the quality of life deteriorate. This goes on while the people downtown are mesmerized by their 10K fantasy.

Some of my neighbors haven't had sleep in months as a result of what hip-hoppers call "the beat," an ear-piercing, nerve-rattling, obnoxious bass, whose sound is amplified by placing speakers in the trunk of one's car. It goes on all day and all night on my street, the kind of torture tactic that was used to flush out Noriega. Dangerous dogs roam through the streets and young women offer their bodies to the residents for money. At one time—before the freeways and urban renewal, before the exportation of manufacturing jobs and integration broke up the African-rooted idea of the extended family that had been handed down through the generations—an adult could get a youngster to obey by threatening the offender with a report to his or her parents. My Yoruba teacher says that in the old culture the greatest threat that you could make to a youngster was "Go home."

For some reason, I'm always finding myself on panels on which I'm forty years older than everybody else. Earlier in the year, I had appeared on a panel called "Hip-Hop and Beyond," held at the University of California, Berkeley. The moderator, a young man who hosts an afternoon hip-hop show on KPFA, attempted to make me a representative of an older generation that had abandoned his generation. I tried to explain that the generational divide was more complicated than that and got screamed at. Some of the hip-hoppers are capable of making entertaining music, but when it comes to political analysis they sound goofy. Someone who has a more thoughtful explanation for what's happened to life in the inner city is former councilman and mayoral candidate Wilson Riles Jr. We interviewed him at the School for Social Justice and Community Development, where he is principal.

We've got buildings that are only thirty percent occupied, and we've got a decline in employment, so as a consequence of that, when our economy goes down, we end up with more crime and more difficulties. More jobs were available two years ago. Now that the bubble has burst, crime has gone up in the country, even in Oakland. I think Jerry [Brown] has had a devastating impact. This month is the first month where we will be looking at more consequences, like the end of welfare checks. We are talking about thousands of people in Oakland who will essentially be pushed out the door, and there won't be an alternative for them. People will end up with serious desperation, and again, the consequence of that is increased crime, divorce, and drug and alcohol use. Jerry tried to put a cap on it by putting one hundred more police officers on the street, a kind of Gestapo thing. I think Brown has made it clear that he doesn't want black leadership in Oakland. He was quoted in the newspapers as saying that one of the things that he wanted to accomplish during his first term was to basically destroy black leadership in his community. Some black people have moved to Antioch and those kinds of places. Black churches have begun to be built in those areas. The housing is somewhat cheaper out there. There clearly is dispersal. Some blacks are going to Sacramento. The Hispanic community has a larger concentration and they double or triple up, so they can stay. We are going to have a decrease in blacks, but the Hispanic and Latino population in Oakland is growing fast, so it won't become an all-white city anytime soon.

Oakland wouldn't have a large black population if it weren't for the Black Panthers. Bobby Seale's election in 1972 turned the city around, got black people voting. Jerry Brown wanted the freeway. That's what attracted him to

Oakland. So he made a deal with the Panthers. Some of the black ministers were mesmerized by the support they got from Brown during his last election. They've been playing footsie with him. But the flatlands were against Jerry Brown. They felt that his idea of turning Oakland around was to bring rich white folks in. And now Brown is on the decline.

As if to confirm Riles's pessimistic assessment, bad news began to appear in the newspapers. Oakland schools were close to bankruptcy as a result of bad fiscal management. The *East Bay Express* revived the scandal that has dogged Jacques Barzaghi, who was accused of sexually harassing women in City Hall, one of whom received a settlement from the city. Brown defended his aide, and seemed to be blaming the women, which is what he accused Bill Clinton of doing when he debated then presidential candidate Clinton during the Democratic primary in New York in 1996.

The administration was suffering from a budgetary crisis, and announced that there would be a cutback on arts funding. Among those groups that would lose funding would be the Black Cowboy Parade and the Blues Society, headed by Ron Stewart.

BLACK MONDAY, APRIL 7, 2003

Brenda Payton described the aftermath of an antiwar demonstration at the Port of Oakland on April 7 in her *Tribune* column of the next day: "There are dozens of unanswered questions about Monday's disastrous police response to anti-war protesters at the Port of Oakland. Chief among them is why officers fired wooden dowels, beanbags, and stinger grenades at a group of largely peaceful protesters." Nine longshoremen who weren't part of the demonstration were also injured. The following week, protesters crowded a meeting of the Oakland City Council to denounce police actions. One Union leader compared it to Nazi repression of the 1930s, but he didn't have to go abroad for an analogy. Albert Vetere Lannon's *Fight or Be Slaves: The History of the Oakland–East Bay Labor Movement* recounts the history of the bloody labor strife that laces Oakland's own history. So rowdy did the Council session become that when Council President Ignacio de la Fuente tried to move the agenda to the next topic; he was shouted down. He had to be escorted from the meeting by the police, but returned later when some women council members insisted the meeting be continued. Mayor Jerry Brown said that he thought the police action was "appropriate." This remark prompted a Union leader to remark that when Brown had his *We the People* show on radio station KPFA, where he posed as a populist in order to woo future voters, he denounced the evil of globalization. Now, as mayor, he had become its chief enforcer.

Of the police response to the protesters, *Chronicle* columnist Chip Johnson wrote, "Oakland police officers responded to an anti-war demonstration outside the Port of Oakland last Monday with a display of force that would have made Bull Connor blush."

April 13, 2003

I woke up with a feeling of disgust and anger today. A few days before, *The New York Times* had run a photo of Iraqi corpses piled high in a morgue. The cause of death was a new version of America's manifest destiny, similar to the kind that nearly exterminated the American Indians, though neocolonial historians attribute this mass murder solely to the Indians' contacting disease (a virus called The Rifle). The doctors were wearing masks in front of the dead bodies of those Iraqis who had been going about their daily lives, minding their own business, when the Pentagon decided make them test cases for new weaponry, cluster bombs, and degraded uranium. The masked doctors were waiting for the victims' relatives to claim their corpses.

And as if the anarchy, chaos, and genocide that the American army had brought to Iraq weren't enough, reports began circulating that the museum at Baghdad had been looted. With the kind of fundamentalist mentality in power in the United States at the moment, I wouldn't be surprised if the treasures of Mesopotamian art were considered expendable because of their pagan imagery. The neo-Confederates who were hawking this war had said that they represented civilization, but after this invasion I was wondering what civilization they were talking about and whether the seat of western civilization was now Crawford, Texas. In the Blues, west Texas represents Hell.

APRIL 26, 2003

Tennessee and I show up at Frank Ogawa Plaza to await the arrival of ILWU members, who are marching from Water Street in Jack London Square to the Plaza in protest of Black Monday. We're about a half hour early and the only others present are the members of the Socialist Workers' Party and a folk singer who will later entertain the rally's audience.

At about 2:30 P.M., we heard some chanting and shouting coming from Broadway, behind where we were sitting on the steps of the Plaza. The marchers turned the corner into Fourteenth Street and a roar went up as they headed toward the Plaza. There were people from all backgrounds included in the march, carrying flags and banners. This was a textbook proletariat march. Unlike the student and peace demonstrations that seemed so white and middle class, this demonstration included whites with a large contingent of blacks and Hispanics. Some on the Left had observed that blacks were missing from the peace demonstrations. Maybe that's because blacks had been betrayed by the Left since the Old Left of the 1930s, a theme of Ellison's *Invisible Man* and Himes's *Lonely Crusade.* David Hilliard and others had complained about their betrayal by the New Left in the 1960s. Apparently, the ILWU had not failed their black members, because not only was the moderator of the ceremonies, union member Clarence Thomas, a black man, but a number of the speakers were black men, rare for a Left demonstration, where usually the only black males on the podium are hip-hop acts and entertainers. Shortly, we were surrounded by the crowds. While speaker after speaker blasted George Bush, the crowd hissed at the mention of Jerry Brown's name. The folk singer, who, with Tennessee, me, and Gus, waited for forty-five minutes for the marchers to arrive, set the tone for the rally. He was wearing a T-shirt that identified George Bush as a terrorist and sang a song with the refrain "George Bush is a moron." The criticism of George Bush was often humorous and cartoonish, but that of Jerry Brown came from anger and disappointment. "When you vote for the lesser of two evils, you always get a Jerry Brown," one speaker said. Some speakers pointed out that Brown and Ignacio de la Fuente would've joined the picket lines in a former time. Now they were on the other side. A vociferous heckler interrupted the proceedings, referring to the protesters as "draft-dodging motherfuckers," but this didn't prevent further criticism of the mayor.

The person who received the most applause at the rally was Sri Louise of San Francisco, one of the victims of the Black Monday attack. When she sat near us, I could see the wounds from her injuries caused by wooden dowels fired by the police. Her neck and jaw were still swollen and marked with huge red blotches. Overshadowed by the police attack on the longshoremen was the reason for the protest in the first place. It was organized by Direct Action to Stop the War to block the gates of SSA and APL, shipping terminals they maintained were profiting from war-related government contracts.

MAY 2, 2003

Deborah Vaughn, artistic director of the popular
Dimensions Dance Theater, appeared on KPFA radio to
announce that an upcoming performance being held by the
thirty-year-old African-American dance troupe might be
their last in the Alice Arts Center. She said that Jerry Brown
wanted to move out the twenty or so community groups
currently occupying the Alice so that he could expand one
of his pet projects, the Arts Academy, in opposition to his
own previous assurances that no such thing would happen.
Why, she asked, would the city want to disrupt the harmo-
nious relationships that have been established between the
different groups so that he could expand an elitist Arts
Academy? In addition to Dimensions Dance Theater, the
facility houses the Axis Dance Company, Bay Area Blues
Society, CitiCentre Dance Theatre, Dance-A-Vision, Dia-
manocura, Moving On Center, and the Oakland Youth
Orchestra. Douglas Allen-Taylor, the brilliant columnist for
the *Berkeley Daily Planet,* wrote: "One wonders if Mayor
Jerry Brown walks through downtown Oakland with his
eyes purposely covered so that he cannot see the people he
insists are just not there."

Some have attributed Oakland's high crime rate to the
fact that young people have little to do. Young people on my
street stand in driveways for hours at a time, fetishizing auto-
mobiles and blasting stereo music so loud that it sounds like
thunder and makes the houses on the street vibrate and nervous systems tremor. A local mechanic had the bright idea

to rig something called a "whistle stick" to car mufflers, which only adds to the cacophony and the miserable quality of life in Oakland's flats. I asked Tennessee to put on some gloves and examine the debris teenagers left behind after a night of performing "sideshows" on our street. She found food from a fast-food joint called Carl's Jr., as well as from McDonald's and KFC—food low in nutrition and high in carbohydrates, fat, sugar, and salt—Skittles candy, and soda with loads of sugar. On May 10, gunshots could be heard in the street in front of our house, which meant that a neighborhood crack house was experiencing internal dissension. During the following week there was a raid on the crack house, but we were used to it and knew that another one would take its place. The administration that says it wants to attract business to Oakland but has difficulty doing so because of the crime rate now wants to evict groups that could actually provide alternate activities for young people. On May 19, Jerry Brown spoke of the idleness among the young people who loitered in front of his condominium on Telegraph Avenue. But his awareness doesn't seem to move him to encourage his developer friends or the downtown corporations to include recreational facilities for young people in their plans.

On May 6, Mayor Brown, who had established himself as a law and order mayor by signaling to the police department that he'd like something done about West Oakland, a largely black neighborhood, and who had endorsed the police actions against the peace demonstrators and long-shoremen, said that he was interested in running for State

Attorney General. "It's something that's come up," Brown told the *San Francisco Chronicle,* "so I've given it some thought. But it's way premature."

JULY 1

Today is the day of the "Tuesday Massacre." Nearly six months after Wilson Riles Jr. said that Mayor Brown wanted to cripple Oakland's black leadership, Oaklanders awoke to the *Oakland Tribune's* shocking headlines: "City Hall Shake-up, Mayor Forces out Bobb, Edwards." The newspaper speculated that the mayor and black city manager Robert Bobb had reached a parting of the ways over development issues (parks commissioner Harry Edwards also resigned). The mayor favored the "uptown" Forest City development, the project favored by Brown's developer friends, while Bobb held out for the construction of a ballpark in that space. On July 5, the *Tribune* said that Jacques Barzaghi, the mayor's mysterious "Svengali," had a hand in the firing of Bobb— another example of this Rasputin's strange power over Brown. Their source said that "Jacques has never gotten over what he believed was Bobb hanging him out to dry" since Barzaghi's sexual harassment case. To complicate matters, Brown's "close friend and developer" John Protopappas was named the new Port Commission president.

In a scathing op-ed that appeared in the *Tribune* on July 7, printed under the head "Brown's Long String of Messes," writer Larry Jackson said that Brown's developer friends and campaign contributors had a hand in Bobb's firing. Jackon's assessment of Brown's tenure as mayor was devastating. He wrote "In the last five years, what has Oakland gained? A national reputation for murder, gangs, thuggery, a failed school system, the Riders lawsuit, the Raiders suit, a relationship with its sports teams that hang by the thread, the gentrification of an entire slice of the city, the wholesale pillage and selloff of the city to Jerry's developer friends."

Chip Johnson's column in the *San Francisco Chronicle,* printed on the same day, was just as acerbic. It was headed "Moonbeam Blew It On Bobb, Firing Bodes Poorly for Mayor's 2nd Term." Of the firing Johnson wrote, "It's the single worst decision he's made in 5½ years as mayor," and Johnson attributed the decision to "the combination of too much ego and meager management skills." Oddly enough, the only support for Brown's firing of Bobb came from a reporter for a local tabloid that sees denigrating black individuals, institutions, and groups as cultivating the same readership market as those who stage "bum fights" for sale to people who enjoy that kind of thing. And KPFA, after ignoring the firing of two prominent black men by Brown (maybe because the people who run the station view racism as a black male problem and they have issues with black men) and devoting space to Hong Kong politics and the fate of the white shark, finally dealt with the matter a week after the story broke by having the tabloid reporter on. He praised Brown for curing Oakland of the "ills of Urban liberalism." *A-hem.*

© Richard Nagler 2003

FIRST ROW, FROM LEFT TO RIGHT: *(kneeling) Jim McKinney, Rusty Allen, James Nelson, Gino; (seated) Jimmy McCraklin, Jay Payton, Ronnie Stewart; (standing) Wiley Trass, Teddy Watson (with cane).*

SECOND ROW, FROM LEFT TO RIGHT: *Henry Clement (standing, in top hat), Finney Mo (wearing cap), Ishmael Reed, Delhart Johnson, Jesse James, "Li'l" Frances, Beverly Stovall, Lady Bianca, Faye Carol, Bobby Reed, Larry Vann, Ronald Wells.*

THIRD ROW, FROM LEFT TO RIGHT: *Lenny Williams, Bill Mabry, Olan Christophper, John Turk, Richard Lewis, Carl Green, Marvin Holmes, Stix, Stanley, Lippett, Big Bob, Bobby Cochran, Kito Gamble, Terrible Tom Bowden.*

A Great Day in Oakland

D URING MY TRIP to New York on March first
through the fifth, my editor, Chris Jackson, and I
discussed the cover of *Blues City*. When I returned to
Oakland, I contacted Ron Stewart of the Oakland Blues
Society to see if perhaps he could help me round up some
blues musicians. I had in mind a shot for the cover that
would resemble the classic *Great Day in Harlem* photo, in
which a number of legendary black jazz musicians posed
together on the steps of a Harlem brownstone. We ended
up using the photo on the facing page. But our conversation
quickly turned to the lack of respect for blues as an art
form. I listened as Stewart told me his story.

*I went to Cole School in West Oakland. Ironically, our block
was the first street in West Oakland to experience urban
renewal. That was in 1962. Urban renewal broke up our tightly*

knit community. This is the truth, Ishmael: Back then adults who didn't know us felt a responsibility to discipline us when we were out of line. Like if we were in the park playing, and if someone would see us messing up, they would say, "I'm going to tell Miss Stewart on you," or they would come over and hit us on the hand and say, "Get home. Get on, boy."

Blues musicians migrated to the South during the [Second World] War to work in the shipyards, and they brought their instruments with them. Seventh Street between Wood and Center Streets, Pine Street, Henry Street, and Camel Street were full of blues. You had the Reno Club and Miss Essie's Place, a very popular club on Wood and Seventh Streets. Essie had hamburgers and a jukebox, and every now and then she'd put a band in there. They had black and white clubs, segregated, but lined up one next to the other. Then they had Pearl Harbor Liquor, which had a jukebox. See, back in those days, there was a whole culture of jukeboxes. They played nothing but blues. One outstanding musician was Saunders King. He played guitar, and he was raised on Seventh Street. He had his first hit back in 1942 and his daughter Deborah is married to Carlos Santana. He was extremely important in the development of the Oakland Blues; the reason the Oakland scene was so popular was because people liked Saunders King and Bob Geddins [a songwriter, producer, and arranger]. Geddins owned three or four record labels and was the first African-American to own one. He owned Big Town Records and Uptown Records. He recorded Jimmy McCracklin, Johnny Hartsman, Lowell Fulson, Roy Hawkins. He even recorded "The Thrill Is Gone," but Modern Records ripped

*him off for that. It ended up being the biggest song of B. B.
King's career. That came out of Oakland in 1949. Jimmy
McCracklin gave the song to Roy Hawkins to sing, and Bob
Geddins was part of that song. The country star Allan Jackson
had a big hit with "Mercury Blues," which was another song
by Bob Geddins and J. C. Douglas [Douglas was another
artist recorded by Geddins]. John Lee Hooker was another
bluesman who came to Oakland. His music was about the
bloodline, and he created the boogie, which is a holy rhythm
that they play in the black churches. Because it's so repetitious,
and sounds like a heartbeat, it's catchy. It makes people jump
around like jackrabbits.*

*Do you remember the Natural Four? They were on Soul
Train and they had four gold records and they came out of
Oakland. They made it to American Bandstand two or
three times, and they were probably the only people besides
Jimmy McCracklin that made it to American Bandstand
during that era from Oakland. That is a feat in itself. They
went to the Apollo four or five times and to every major TV
show that was out there. They had a lot of great hits.*

*I got a fourteen-thousand-dollar development grant to cre-
ate a Walk of Fame [for Oakland blues history]. The Walk of
Fame will honor people like Paul Reed of Reed's Record
Shop and Raincoat Jones, who got his name because he came
to Oakland with just a raincoat. He was a gambler who
funded a whole lot of clubs. Of course the Walk is going to
have Slim Jenkins and Esther Mayberry. You know, there used
to be a time when the arts were as important in Oakland as
they are in New Orleans and Memphis. Those cities built a*

whole growth industry off of their blues. Oakland got away from that and wanted to fund all of the visual artists. Last month a white guy had just released a CD and he called up and told me that he called it West Coast, Bay Area Blues, but there was no black guys on it. I forget his name. Do you know what he told me? He said that he couldn't find any blacks. He wanted me to write a couple of paragraphs for his liner notes, and I refused to do it.

I was one of the cochairs of Jerry Brown's entertainment committee for his inaugural, but I think I made a mistake because all of the things that I wanted to do I didn't get any funding for. My aim was to bring in groups like the Natural Four and Lenny Williams, groups that would have never had an opportunity to be a part of the inaugural. I wanted to show people all over the world that Jerry was the new mayor. But we got nothing. It went to others. The California Music Awards came to Oakland two years ago. They got red-carpet treatment and didn't do shit. They got about sixty or seventy grand from the city. I just did my Hall of Fame Show and I didn't get one penny. I was told that they didn't have any money. When the other show came to town we called and we said, "Look, how can you come to Oakland and take Oakland's money? Here are all these taxpaying citizens of Oakland and you've got all of these white people on the show, no blacks." All they had was the Sea Biscuits, some black rap group or something. I called up the California Music Awards and I said, "You gonna have people picketing this show if we don't have no representation." They said, "What do you want to do?" And I said, "I want to play a couple of *songs that are indigenous to Oakland because other than that you got all of these white people performing who don't even live here."* So the Blues Society performed and we kicked ass. Everybody like Channel Seven, Santana, and Huey Lewis said that we were great.

[*I asked him what he thought of Jimmy McCracklin's remark that black kids aren't as interested in the blues as white kids.*]

I hate for black people to make that comment. If you were a carpenter and you built a house with wood, why the hell would you just be a wood carpenter when everyone is building with stucco? If all of the opportunities went to white kids then why should black people write the blues when the promoters, record companies, and agencies are run by whites? Why should black youth venture into blues when they can do hip-hop? They can make more money. They can make a living.

But now Oakland is not the most popular blues. Chicago blues, Delta blues, and Texas blues are probably more popular. The musicians moved on. Some of them changed their style of music. But there is still a blues presence in Oakland. There are still musicians playing. The blues, in a sense, defines Oakland. The blues is an art form, but it's also about a lifestyle, and there are still a lot of songs. You write about what happened to you, you write about your landlord, you write about gentrification. Bo Diddley got a song about the eagle ["My Eagle Is Pissed," a jingoistic song about war*] and all of this stupid shit. I wasn't too fond of it, the eagle being mad. Oakland's a city that's got blues, in a sense.*

To be honest, I'd say that Jerry Brown is not trying to get rid of the black people in Oakland. Anybody is good to Jerry Brown if they have money. If they don't earn more than seventy thousand dollars a year then they are of no use to him. You heard about them closing down Sweet Jimmy's [a popular black nightclub located in Oakland's downtown], right? I told the city that we should put a blues club in the Fox Theatre. I said that everybody forgot about blues when the individual artists came in. Oakland was famous not for paintings but for the blues. There is a strange twist in the funding. They would rather give it to visual artists, gay pride parades, or African art than to African-American art. We started a series called Swan's Blues Songs as part of the Swan's Marketplace [a mixed-use development in Old Oakland]. The lady that worked there when we started the series quit. The new woman told me that I had to write her a proposal [to keep the series]. I said that I was not going to kiss her ass and jump through her hoops. This was a white lady. When you go to Chinatown they have more sponsors [for their arts] than everyone else. They had people that I didn't know gave money. I went to Safeway and Sears and they told me to go fuck myself. The Oakland Blues Society has a subscribership of three or four thousand. All of these white assholes don't want to help us but we are the only black organization like this in the United States. People say that the Oakland blues has died, but it hasn't.

MARCH 12, 2003

As if to confirm Stewart's statement, musicians from several generations showed up for our shoot in front of Esther's

Orbit Room, the last of the old-time blues clubs located on the legendary Seventh Street. Richard Nagler, the photographer, kept shaking his head and saying, "This is great; this is great." I was so surprised that I stuttered while attempting to address the crowd and inform them that the photo was to be in my book *Blues City*. Someone asked me to sit in the center of the photo and I demurred. I told them that I knew my place. I felt honored enough to have Little Jimmy Scott, Bobby Womack, Taj Mahal, and Eddie Harris sing some lyrics I'd written, but nobody in this crowd knew or cared about that. They ranked themselves. "Let him sit up front," they'd say about a fellow performer. But we got through it. They were patient as Richard tried to get the best possible photograph. After the shoot, I bought everybody a drink inside Esther's. She showed up about a half hour after the photos had been taken, dressed in her finery.

She asked me to stay for a chicken dinner they were all having. The sun finally came out, after an overcast day with clouds threatening rain. But it hadn't rained. Perfect light for the blues. Overcast, dreary, but ultimately, sunny. On this day, we forgot about Oakland's intractable problems.

The Universe

BEFORE WRITING THIS book, my knowledge of Oakland was like that of the early astronomers of the universe. The universe was a small neighborhood of my concerns, and I had very little knowledge of the goings-on outside of the center of the block on which I live. My routine usually took me to the university and, perhaps three times a week, for walks around the Emeryville marina, from where I could gaze out on the bay and on clear days see Alcatraz and the ocean beyond the Golden Gate Bridge. In fact I live on the border between Oakland and Emeryville, and my post office is located in Emeryville, a booming city where gambling is legal. If I hadn't written this book, I would not have become acquainted with Oakland's many worlds. Nor would I have met the many volunteers, the true heroes and heroines of the city who strive to keep the heritage of Oakland alive in the face of fierce and often malevolent forces of development. There were surprises, too. I was instructed during the

Black Panther tour that some of the key landmarks of the Panther history are located in my neighborhood and that Bobby Seale lives a few blocks from me. Author Amy Tan once lived in this neighborhood.

We began our Oakland tour at the foot of Oakland and ended in a place where there is no end in sight. From the waterfront where Jack London and his associates got into drunken brawls to a building that houses Einstein's telescope, where one can look through any of three telescopes and gaze at a universe that is flying off into God knows where.

Tennessee and I drive to Thirty-fifth Avenue, exit off 580 from Oakland. We turn left and for about twenty minutes drive to 1000 Skyline Boulevard, the site of the Chabot Space & Science Center. The architect of record was Gerson/Overstreet. Harry Overstreet, our family friend, is the son of novelist Cleo Overstreet and brother of Joe Overstreet, the artist and owner of New York's Kenkeleba Gallery.

Much of the funding for Chabot came from the defense budget. Congressman Dellums shepherded the proposal through the House, and Councilman Dick Sprees' son, then a clerk on the Appropriations Committee, also helped. Sprees himself was pivotal to getting the funding. The proposal was included in a line item totaling $18 million attached to a defense bill. The city of Oakland provided the land, and the schools provided some telescopes. Governors Pete Wilson and Gray Davis provided $6 million. Ask Jeeves, the search engine company, donated $2.5 million for the planetarium, and the megadome theater was funded by the late Chancellor Tien of U.C. Berkeley. To prevent damage to all the buildings in case of an earthquake, the space center was built in segments. The planetarium seats 243; the science theater seats 210 and features a state-of-the-art megasystem projector; the Challenger Learning Center replicates NASA missions; and the Chabot Observatory watches the sky.

The "captain" who runs the mock space station tells us that Sprees followed the development of the center from the first shovel of dirt. At the age of seventy-four, the councilman is stepping down from District 4. Sprees grew up on a farm outside of Oregon City, Oregon, and did graduate work at Georgetown University after a stint in the air force during the Korean War. A Republican, he was first elected to office in 1979. Vice president of public affairs for Kaiser Aluminum & Chemical Corporation for thirty-one years, Sprees retired in 1987. He told the *San Francisco Chronicle* columnist Chip Johnson that he considers the Chabot Space & Science Center his highest achievement.

Sprees greets Tennessee and me at the rotunda located at the entrance. The rotunda includes pillars that are supposed to represent Stonehenge. At the solstices, sunlight lines up with arrows located on the floor. Also included in the rotunda is a model of the space station and television monitors that show the activity at NASA. Chabot is affiliated with both NASA and the Smithsonian. We enter the planetarium, where a Zeiss projector produces the exact model for ninety-four hundred stars and the fourteen-thousand–watt surround-sound system produces perfect sound, according to Sprees. Each star has its own light source. Sprees tells us that there are two others in the world like it, one at the Hayden Planetarium in New York. He says that he wanted the planetarium to be first-class. "In this planetarium, we can travel three thousand years into the future and three thousand years into the past. We can travel out to one of the planets and look at Earth." Tennessee and I sit with Dick Sprees in the planetarium as above us ninety-four hundred stars whirl about the Milky Way, the music lulling us into the sense that we are actually out there. This experience would be hard to duplicate.

After touring the classrooms and the mock Challenger space station, after crossing a sky bridge to the Dellums building from the Sprees building, Tennessee and I join Sprees in watching a movie in the Tien MegaDome Theater. It shows an exploration of the inner body, and Tennessee finds it hard to take at certain points. After watching the stomach break down foods like some sort of washing machine, I vow to chew my food more carefully. The next morning, while swimming at the YMCA, I see myself as a movie skeleton moving through the waters, an image triggered by having watched movie skeletons moving about in everyday activities the day before. The Chabot Center is a gigantic, transformative teaching tool; when you exit you're not the same person who entered.

Dick Sprees says that the observatory's purpose is to show students and the public where one is in the universe. At one time astronomers believed that nothing existed outside of our solar system. Hubble Space Telescope pictures on display show galaxies upon galaxies, somewhat like our experiences with a village, town, and city. Most of us spend our lives viewing our environment through a haze, but if we work hard enough, the haze lifts and the view becomes limitless.

DEDICATED CITIZENS WILL continue to insist that the Oakland skyline remains honest. They will be contested by mayors like Carpentier and Brown who are hell-bent on developing every square inch and malling over the city's history. Just as the mission padres discouraged any enthusiasm for Indian culture, Carpentier tried to end bullfighting, the sport of the Californios. And the number one artistic export of Oakland, the blues, is disrespected. Ron Stewart may not get respect from the philistines who run the city's arts budgets, but the Scots had enough reverence for the blues to bring his group to Scotland and house them in a castle. Just as the enormous profits from gold made for hazardous living in northern California, the profits of crack capitalism will cause the crime rate to peak and fall cyclically. During the port strike, the death rate decreased. As an ex-councilwoman told me, illegal drugs couldn't be unloaded since ships were stalled in the estuary.

Lothario Lotho, a Blues impresario, said that Oakland was a Blues City, because in Oakland there is no hope. But despite the crime rate, the failing schools, the ambitious politicians who use the city like a woman for a one-night stand only to forget about her the next day, I have tried to show in this book that a certain class and dignity—even majesty—emerges from Oakland's history. For every crack thug and every selfish regentrifier there are people like Esther's Orbit Room founder, the late Bill Mabry. He died shortly after posing for our blues photo; he'd bought a new suit especially for the photo session. While Oakland has been beset by taxpayer-subsidized developers who are so ruthless that they make the landlords in the old New Masses cartoons seem like Salvation Army volunteers, Mabry offered rooms to people who had no place to live and gave a break to people who couldn't come up with the rent. Yes, there is the violent side of Oakland, the uncivil types who have little regard for the feelings of their fellow citizens and neighbors, but Bill Mabry represents the true spirit of Oakland. So did my late neighbor David McClure, the man they called "the Gum Man." David used to buy chewing gum wholesale and give it away to the crowds of children who would amass at his front door every morning. A year after his death, children would still come around, looking for the Gum Man. As I said in the eulogy I delivered at his funeral, he didn't wear his Christianity like a fur coat, he practiced it. The same could be said of Mother Wright, Mary Wright, Sisters Maureen and Caroline, and the many volunteers who spend every day repairing wrecked lives. Who refute the upscale social Darwinists by showing that there is as much cooperation in life as there is competition. Indeed, there is evidence that in nature animals look out for other animals who aren't even members of their species. What does that say about us? What does that say about

Berkeley and San Francisco, where you can witness people dying in the street? Jack London, who was raised by a black woman, would be in a rage. He would write a wild angry stream of invective about such disregard for the poor. When London cussed out those New York capitalists, he was speaking for Oakland.

And no matter the future of Oakland, the beauty of the place will remain. A beauty captured by African-American poet William Nauns Ricks in his 1902 poem, *Night in California:*

> *When the sun is sinking slow*
> *Behind the mountains blue and white*
> *And the mist upon the town is falling low*
> *When the mocker's sleepy note*
> *Seems to stifle in his*
> *throat*
> *Then to us in California, it is night*

Acknowledgments

Thanks to Annalee Allen, Ron Stewart, Denise Lewis, David Hilliard, William Wong, Mary Jo Wainright, Holly Alonso, Wilson Riles Jr., Rose and David Berreyesa, Chuck Striplin, Rupert Garcia, Lothario Lotho, Bill Mabry, and especially Tennessee Reed, whose assistance was invaluable.

About the Author

*I*SHMAEL REED has written nine novels, four books of poetry, five plays and four books of essays and numerous anthologies. He is the editor of *Konch* and *Vines*, *The International Student Anthology*, both available at www.ishmaelreedpub.com. His songs have been performed and recorded by Taj Mahal, Eddie Harris, Bobby Womack, Little Jimmy Scott, and Mary Wilson. He has been nominated for two National Book Awards. Recent awards include the Lila Wallace-Reader's Digest Award, and a John D. and Catherine T. MacArthur Foundation Fellowship. In 2001, he received a Chancellor's Award for Community Service. In 2003, he received the Barnes and Noble Writer for Writers Award and the Phillis Wheatley Award from the Harlem Book Fair. He has been a senior lecturer at the University of California at Berkeley since 1968.

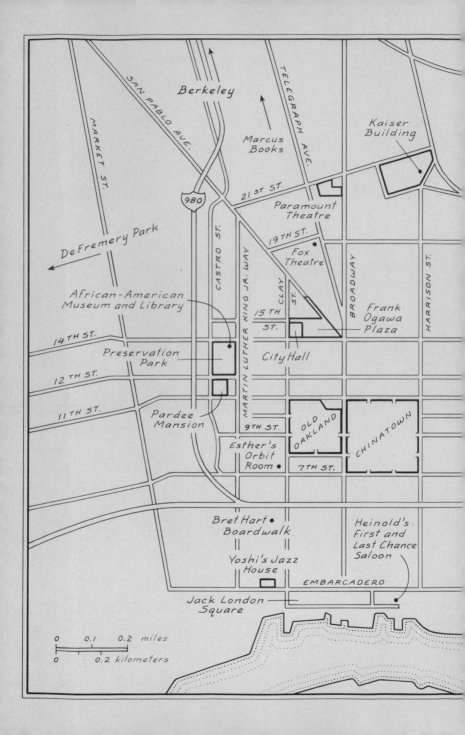

Berkeley

MARKET ST.

SAN PABLO AVE.

TELEGRAPH AVE.

Kaiser Building

Marcus Books

980

21ST ST.

Paramount Theatre

DeFremery Park

19TH ST.

CASTRO ST.

Fox Theatre

CLAY ST.

MARTIN LUTHER KING JR. WAY

BROADWAY

HARRISON ST.

African-American Museum and Library

15TH ST.

Frank Ogawa Plaza

14TH ST.

Preservation Park

City Hall

12TH ST.

11TH ST.

OLD OAKLAND

CHINATOWN

Pardee Mansion

9TH ST.

Esther's Orbit Room

7TH ST.

Bret Hart Boardwalk

Heinold's First and Last Chance Saloon

Yoshi's Jazz House

EMBARCADERO

Jack London Square

0   0.1   0.2 miles

0   0.2 kilometers